The Footprints of God

The Footprints of God

The Relationship of
Astrology, C.G. Jung, and the Gospels

Luella Sibbald

Guild for Psychological Studies
Publishing House
San Francisco, California

Published in the United States of America by
The Guild for Psychological Studies Publishing House
2230 Divisadero Street
San Francisco, California 94115

Second Printing September 1989

Cover Design and Astrological Chart—Dorothy Nissen
Typesetting—Pan O'Sea Typesetters, Waldport, Oregon
Printing—Delta Lithograph Co., Valencia, California

Library of Congress Cataloging in Publication Data

Sibbald, Luella, 1907 -
   The Footprints of God
   1.Astrology. 2. Astrology and psychology. 3. Jung,
C.G. (Carl Gustav), 1875-1961. 4. Jesus Christ—Teach-
ings—Miscellanea. I. Title.
BF1711.S5 1988   133.5   88-32010

ISBN 0-917479-11-4

TO
ELIZABETH BOYDEN HOWES
AND
SHEILA MOON
WITH
DEEP GRATITUDE

Table of Contents

Foreword

The words, "the Aquarian Age," first caught my attention when I was a teenager. The years until that age would come seemed an eternity to me. I had no expectation I would reach it, but I wanted to know more about it.

The phrases I heard: "an individual in community," "all persons being treated with respect and dignity," "the flow of Living Water from those who are ready to receive it"—were what made a deep impression on me. I found few interested people to talk with about it. Many to whom I brought it completely dismissed astrology. At that time I did not find anything written about the Ages.

When I was in Zurich the first time in 1948 working with Toni Wolff, I mentioned having been interested at one time in astrology. In answering her question of how I expressed my interest now, I said that I had just let it drop. Her reply indicated it was not wise to let former interests drop back into the unconscious.

I saw Dr. Jung for one individual hour

while there and asked him about the Aquarian Age. In his intuitive wisdom he began with something far more personal. I have always been grateful for what he chose to talk about. That one hour was extremely important to me at that particular time. I still didn't know about the Aquarian Age.

In 1955 when I returned to Zurich I worked on astrology with Gret Baumann-Jung, and I returned more often after to work with her. Her warmth of personality and wealth of knowledge about her work made every hour a wonderful experience.

Sometime in the late sixties she told me one could draw a chart that could indicate the qualities of each age that had passed and the Aquarian Age to come. I was delighted to have my questions answered, and it was satisfying to know that some of this knowledge could be known to a certain extent by using the chart. I am indebted to Gret Baumann for this explanation and had so hoped she would publish it with the interesting material she had accumulated. My concern and interest has made this part of astrology exceedingly important to me.

In the meantime another subject of interest had arisen. I was teaching in San Francisco when a friend told me of her experience at a seminar she attended the year before in the mountains of southern California. They studied the Synoptic Gospels, she told me, in a seminar based on the *Records of the Life of Jesus*, discerning what could be authentic and what was mythic or what was added later about the life and teachings of Jesus. I went immediately to a seminar that summer of 1945.

A modified Socratic method of leaders' questions and the individual answers of the seminarees was a new experience then. Each person determined from the discussion which answer seemed right to him/her. What I learned from the method as well as about the teachings of Jesus gripped me more than anything else had in my life or since. That was over forty years ago, and I have been in touch with that material or leading it during every year since.

The method was used first by Dr. Henry B. Sharman, who edited the book used there, *The Records of the Life of Jesus*. The method and the seminars were carried on by Dr. Elizabeth Howes after attending Dr. Sharman's seminars for four years. She has continued to work on this material for over fifty years, leading the seminars and continually having new insights for advanced seminars and training new leaders. There are about twenty-five new leaders now leading seminars with the Guild for Psychological Studies in San Francisco and in the place for the seminars, known as Four Springs. The move to this site in northern California occurred in 1956. Previously, seminars were held at the Pines in southern

California. The program has been effectively extended since those early times at the Pines and people from nearly every state, including Alaska and Hawaii, as well as from five or six foreign countries have been participants—some several times.

I had been through the *Records* material many times before I knew about the chart for the Aquarian Age. That was a deep and important experience when I realized that Jesus, through his teaching and life, was the prototype of the Aquarian person. He was not to be an object of worship; but through the life he lived, he taught a way that brought Life. To follow that way would not be an imitation of Jesus; but allows each one to apply the teachings to him/herself.

The evolutionary thrust of the Aquarian Age was what Jesus was living. More will be said about this in the fifth chapter of this book. What one learns and knows about oneself through Jungian analysis is a central way toward becoming a mature person. That is what the Aquarian Age speaks of: to find Life, as Jesus says it, or to become the individuated person in the Jungian way. The truths that one understands from reading Jung carry the same essence of truth that Jesus was talking about.

In 1978 I had published a small booklet containing material on these three subjects, astrology, C.G. Jung, and the Gospels. It was mostly for the leaders of the Guild and people who at-

tended seminars. This present book certainly
relates to all three subjects in content. The fact of
the Aquarian Age is emphasized, as is the importance of knowing about the life and teachings of
Jesus of Nazareth as preparation to live in that
Age.

Three has always been an important number
in my life so it is not surprising that this third
subject is extremely important to me: the depth
psychology of C.G. Jung. After my first *Records*
group in 1945, I realized how little I knew about
my unconscious, my dreams, my inner world in
general.

Soon after, I began Jungian analysis. As I
was reading Jung, I found so many things he
talked about carried the same essence of truth as
did many of Jesus' statements. They were each
speaking a truth. It also became evident that the
Aquarian person is not truly Aquarian in most
cases without knowing about the whole psyche—
conscious and unconscious. The integration of
individuals in the New Age indicates how much
each one is a true citizen of the Aquarian Age.

One thing seems to be a help in that area.
Some people even now are feeling it is necessary
to know more about why they carry so much
anger, or why they have so much anxiety, or so
many obsessions or complexes; others begin to
feel the necessity to know more of themselves.
Furthermore, the children being born seem to be
older souls coming to the planet ready to act on

the truthful material communicated to them in this new era of communication. In talking to teenagers or even younger children I find they seem to understand the importance of real relationship. This is where the emphasis will be in the New Age rather than on work, as it has been in the Piscean Age. That will become clear as you read the book.

When I finished the fifth chapter, which is about Jesus as the Aquarian person, I had written what I wanted this book to contain. However, I had not stressed the importance of the individual chart, so I have included a sixth chapter.

The sixth chapter is a lecture I gave at an astrology conference held on the island of Hawaii in 1978. I was asked to give the lecture as it is expressed in the title, "How I Use Astrology as a Psychotherapist." It was printed in *The American Theosophist*, Fall 1978, as were all the lectures of that conference. It is not an integral part of the first five chapters, so it can be read first, last, or left out entirely. It does help one to understand why people want an astrological chart drawn up and interpreted and why Dr. Jung said it was one of the most important tools to understand oneself.

The biblical references in this book are from the ERV, the English Revised Version, except where noted. The Guild Publishing House is soon to publish the *Records'* format in the Revised Standard Version. That may be more acceptable to some.

Acknowledgments

I want to express special thanks to those who helped to guide *The Footprints of God* to completion.

Florence Little gave much time in the formation of this book out of her years of experience and her great literary knowledge. She was invaluable in her counsel, corrections, suggestions that enlivened certain sections, and editing along the way. Her concern in wanting a final reading moved me very much.

Janet Thompson Petroni did the first typing but did not have time to continue. She made some very important suggestions at the beginning. I was grateful that Gretchen Morgane could become the main typist and was so very valuable.

I appreciated that John Petroni read the book as a whole, making some encouraging comments and corrections. He was especially helpful in corrections connected with the Hebrew Scriptures.

The D.H. Lawrence quote, which fit so well at the end of Chapter V, was thoughtfully sent by Bill Dols.

Before I started writing the book, Charles Pfeifer gave me *The Universe Is a Green Dragon* by Brian Swimme. Reading that book made it possible for me to express the intentionality in the universe out of which come the Ages about which I had felt strongly.

Finally, I am deeply indebted to Karen Carlton for her thorough editing of the whole book, which brought about a greater flow in the material. This was contributed by her in the midst of a very busy professional life, growing out of her concern for the significance of how the fields of interest in the book are woven together.

Without the continual support and encouragement of Elizabeth Howes and Sheila Moon this book probably would not have been written. To them both I express deepest thanks for their loving friendship and support. Elizabeth Howes gave a great deal of time along the way, reading, making suggestions, correcting and helping me understand the significance of this book.

Berkeley   Luella Sibbald
May 1988

THE MEANING OF A NEW AGE: COSMIC EVOLUTION

Chapter One

As we enter the closing years of this twentieth century, we are plunged into an era that could hardly have been imagined when the century began. Our planet is changing at a rate more rapid than has ever been seen before, with its complexity reflected in new ways of perceiving, observing, and thinking. The emerging technological consciousness requires us to master new knowledge, a new global language of computers. Communications systems allow us to reach around the world in a matter of minutes, while air transportation can take us anywhere on the planet in only a few hours. Despite this seeming connectedness amongst peoples and countries of the world, we are lost. We do not know our place in this fast-moving society. We don't know where to find our rootedness. Where is this feeling of wholeness that we long for, this oneness with the rest of the planet, or even with the people next door? We need some insight.

Modern physics tells us that long ago the universe was one great fire. Burning since the beginning of time, unseen and unknown, it radiated a consuming light. Then this primal fireball exploded, sending pieces in all directions, expanding the universe, and populating space. These particles of fire cooled into different forms, becoming different realities—stars, planets, and primitive life. The forms grew more complex, the realities more varied, until human consciousness was born. This single energetic event of the great fireball produced all matter and mind—all life and intelligence. It can be said that everything is made of stardust.

Because the universe began as one great fire, this pattern of wholeness lives in the psyches of human beings. The light of the fireball is all around us as well as inside us. But why do we not feel this oneness? Why are we not in touch with this event and the Source out of which it emerged?

Humankind has not always suffered so fragmented a consciousness. Six thousand years ago people built stone circles to worship their gods, and life reflected a primal oneness. Built on the telluric currents, or places where strong earth energies converge, these stone circles remind us that ancient peoples were together with each other and the earth. Even today these currents can be felt by a person who is in tune with the past and who is capable of living into the sacredness of such places as Stonehenge. But it does not take great sensitivity to know that we have strayed far from the sense of oneness that once was—that sense of oneness with the universe and with the Source from which it comes.

In looking at television, listening to the radio, and reading newspapers or current magazines, we often find references to "a new era of history," "a new age," "a new patterning of energy," "a great change in thinking, language and mores," and "a moving toward the coming of the Aquarian Age."

What are these phrases telling us? They each seem to be expressing something about a time of change that will be both positive and difficult. We see much about us that is anything but positive: threats of nuclear war, huge national and international deficits, crime and terrorism in most countries, uprisings among certain factions in each country. There is much questioning about established institutions, such as the labor movement, the church, the interlocking multinational corporations, and government itself. Some of the questionings and changes that are prevalent have a regressive pull to times past, as is seen in the fundamentalist thinking which dominates large segments of populations in both Western and Eastern countries.

Despite these difficult signs, we must remember that no forward movement can take place in the psyche, the inner world, or in the outer world, without having old habits, mores, and patterns rise up and say, "These changes toward newness, inner and outer, cannot be." The pull of the status quo is demanding. Chaos, confusion, and fear are in the psyches of most people, causing them to retreat to what they feel is the safety of old ways of thinking and living. Unfortunately, this fear and confusion are projected into the outer world, intensifying the difficulties of the times and adding to the already abundant destruction of life and institutions.

But what about the positive side of this time of change, this new age? How do we learn to accept the fear that is in us, as well as much more that is negative, so that our attitudes can be transformed and cease to contaminate the outer world? For it seems very clear that what we do not know about ourselves or accept about ourselves is projected onto people or situations, leaving us locked into feelings of opposition rather than liberated into oneness.

Jung once said that humans know much about many things but next to nothing about themselves. Frustrated by the inevitable destructiveness that accompanies the lack of self knowledge, he spent his life trying to understand more about the human psyche and its relation to the divine. Jung built on Freud's rediscovery of the unconscious, showing that humans *can* know something of themselves. A new quality of consciousness, indeed a new quality of human life, is truly possible. We are only beginning to know something of what will be the evolutionary change in human consciousness. This is the positive side of the new age.

So we see that now is the time to begin to develop this side of our human potential—this inner life of which Jung speaks. After three and a half million years of human development, we are ready to recognize the meaning of that primal fireball which marked our beginnings. We are ready to understand it as an image of wholeness in our psyches, as a symbol of our imagination and creativity, as our connection to the Source. No longer do we need to enumerate our outer achievements, for they are reflected in all forms of science, transportation, and communication. It is time to look at what our inner worlds contain for us; it is time to dig deeply for the gold, the treasure, and the buried cities that are within.

There is an ancient myth that says the Sun follows the footsteps of God. The footsteps are the signs of the Zodiac. With each footstep into a new sign of the Zodiac, the ritual, dogma, and form of religion change. When this mythic statement came into being, all of life centered around the gods or God. To say, then, that religious forms changed was to say that *all of life changed.* It appears today that many of the concrete patterns of life are changing and will change with the "new footsteps of God."

The material in this book will enlarge on the meaning of the "footsteps of God." Emphasis will be given to the "footstep" we are emerging from, that is, the Piscean Age of the last two thousand years, and to the footstep of the Aquarian Age which will take us into the next two thousand years.

Because astrology is central to my thinking in the chapters ahead, I would like to say something about its history and usefulness. As an ancient body of knowledge, astrology came into being long before written language, when truths were gained by direct revelation or by intuitive receptiveness to the wisdom of nature. Some records have been found on tablets as early as the six hundreds BCE. A school of astrology was started on the Island of Cos in 280 BCE by a priest of Baal. We know that Pythagoras studied astrology in Egypt from 569 to 470 BCE, Paracelsus explored it in the fifteenth century CE, and Nostradamus, in the sixteenth century CE, established a relationship between medicine and astrology.

Astrology assumes that the universe, including the earth we live on, is a whole, that there is a correlation between what is above and below, between the stars and human experience. Correlations, and therefore patterns, can be found for everything, pointing to the fact that there are no islands in the universe. We are. And we are one.

Each phenomenon, from the smallest atom to the great galaxies, is shaped by a pattern which, in turn, is born out of the interaction of massive forces in the universe. On a smaller scale, the patterns of a person's life are influenced by the interaction of solar bodies, particularly at the moment of his or her birth. We can say, then, that everything in nature has its pattern, as does every moment of time. It may not be long before facets of nature now unknown to us may reveal themselves. Through the evolving consciousness of humankind we may better understand how astrology functions. We may better receive the unknown energies which are with us now but which we have not yet the consciousness to engage and name.

Asked if I believe in astrology, I would have to say yes. For I cannot otherwise explain how a person's astrological chart, which shows exactly where the planets were in the Zodiac at the time of birth, can so accurately and authentically reflect that person's psyche. C.G. Jung said that astrology "represents the summation of all the psychological knowledge of antiquity." It is no surprise, then, that he often emphasized the importance of *experiencing* one's astrological chart and thereby using it as a tool for understanding one's self.

Jung also said that the patterning in one's psyche is a synchronistic event. The pattern of a specific moment of time is registered in the psyche of each person at the moment of birth. The uniqueness of that moment of time, encountered with the first breath of the newborn child, is imprinted—patterned—in the infant's psyche, never to be repeated.

This patterning in the psyche is revealed on the birth chart, which shows exactly where the planets were in space at the time of birth and what their positions are according to the Zodiac. Taking the names of the Roman gods, these planets function as the archetypes in the collective unconscious. In astrology, the planets, the gods, and archetypes all speak of the same thing. It is clear that the astrological chart is a map of psychological forces which, if read creatively, can give one the choice of acquiescing to what the planets indicate or mastering particularly difficult energies to find the potential that is in one's psyche. That is, one can give in to the fate of one's pattern or one can work toward individuation, which is what Jung called finding our wholeness.

There are some misleading ideas about astrology. Some people think that it preordains one's life, so to speak; by knowing the negative things about oneself, one contributes to their inevitability. But astrology does not make prediction, even though some may try to misuse it that way. Nor are there negative attitudes in the chart that cannot be altered or changed if worked with in a committed way. Alan Leo, the person who really revived the use of astrology at the end of the nineteenth century, said, "The wise man rules his chart; the fool follows it." Jung expressed the same idea in a different way: "To master your chart leads to individuation."

The myth upon which astrology stands is the Twelve Labors of Heracles. In each of the twelve houses of the Zodiac there is a labor that must be met. The first house represents the ego. It shows one's personality, how one feels about one's self, and what others see in us. This first house and the house where the sun falls are very important to master. That is to say, they require our inner-most attention to see if they need more work for transformation, if negative, or for greater expression, if positive.

Not only is it important for an individual to master these two particular houses; it is also important for people to understand and assume responsibility for what is revealed of the collective tasks in the chart of any given age. It must be remembered that astrology serves us both individually and collectively, in the moment and for all of time. Thus, we speak of the tasks of the Piscean Age or the Aquarian Age as well as of those tasks presented to us in our individual charts. Following this chapter will be a discussion of various astrological ages and the collective tasks which accompany them. But first I would like to reflect briefly on the elements as they function in astrology—particularly that of fire, since it symbolizes our consciousness or that which can be developed when one works with the planets/gods/archetypes in one's birth chart.

All life is connected to land, air, and water. In astrology, the elements fire, earth, air, and water are important, with each sign of the Zodiac representing one of the elements. Some of the life in the animal, bird, and insect world move in one element. Some are at home in two elements. Few living things can move in three elements. And no animal, besides humans, can cope with fire. Only humankind can deal with fire both in its destructive and transformative states. Fire is our consciousness.

Greek myth tells us that Prometheus stole a brand of holy fire from the immortal forges to bring to earth. He risked his freedom to give humans this added element which is such a powerful force for both destruction and transformation. Furious that fire had been stolen from the gods, Zeus had Prometheus lashed to a rock with indestructible chains. An eagle fed on his liver every day. As much as was eaten grew back each night, so that Prometheus suffered constantly. Finally, after thirty years of agony, Prometheus was rescued by Heracles, who slew the eagle and broke the chains.

This story of Prometheus suggests the pain our freedom can bring us when we choose to go against the plan of the gods, or the pattern of the archetypes. But it also tells of the transformations that can occur when one dares to rule the chart rather than follow it, mastering the pattern rather than succumbing to it. The God beyond the gods needs us to fulfill our potential, to find that which wants expression in us, even if it means suffering and loss. Indeed, it is often a serious illness, a handicap, or an emotional trauma that wakes us to greater inner capabilities that need expression, that invites us to be responsible for the gods in our psyches.

In bringing fire to humans, Prometheus brought them consciousness. He brought them power from the gods, something uniquely divine. On the positive side, fire is related to our vitality for life, our creative passions, and our will to do the will of God. On the negative side, however, fire is related to our self-will, our will to control and take power. When loosed for selfish and ego-centric purposes, fire is a destructive element, of course. And this is where we are now—facing the destructive creations of a human consciousness out of touch with the will of God.

Long ago, the myth tells us, much of the world was destroyed by water. Then God made a covenant with Noah that the earth would not be flooded again. The rainbow continues to appear. But now it seems that the Earth faces destruction by another element, coming from the Earth rather than the heavens, from humans rather than God. The question presses: Are we equal to risking our lives so that destruction will not come by fire next time?

Yes.

From the Piscean Age of the last two thousand years we are now moving into the Aquarian Age. From Pisces the water sign we are moving to Aquarius the air sign. Because the element that directs each Age demands certain changes and growth, we may look to air, and all that it symbolizes, for help in preventing world destruction by fire. Movements and changes in the human psyche over the centuries continue in our own day and generation. Thus we may hope that the fire of consciousness can be made whole by the air of spirit.

How do we know that we are entering a new astrological age? First it should be remembered that the astrological Zodiac is an abstract division of the sphere of space around us into twelve different segments or signs, Aries through Pisces. These twelve signs, following the order of the twelve constellations seen in the sky, reflect patterns of human characteristics and human activity. The Zodiac is also described as a "band extending about 8 degrees on each side of the ecliptic," which is the great circle from which the Earth views the sun. It is through this band that the Earth receives that which is given to it by the sun and planets.

The movement of each sign of the Zodiac into the place opposite the Vernal Equinox is known as the Precession of the Equinox. The complete precession of the signs on the ecliptic covers a period of time approximately 25,920 years, which is the time it takes the pole of the Earth's axis to complete an entire circle around the pole of the ecliptic. This circle is made by an oscillating movement that is much like that of a spinning top with a swinging motion resembling a nod, called nutation. The unequal gravitational pull of the Sun and the Moon on the Earth's equatorial area causes the swinging motion. Because of this gyration, the position toward which the pole points is called the Pole Star, with a different Pole Star moving into place about every 5,000 years. The present Pole Star is Polarus.

Because of the Precession of the Equinox which was first determined by Hipparchus, around 134 BCE, the signs do not now correspond to the constellations of the same name. In fact, the movement of the sign is backward from the end of the constellation to its beginning. The thirty degrees containing the next sign of the Zodiac move into the equatorial sign in the same way. For example, after Aries being in one position, we might expect Taurus to take its place. However, it is Pisces that enters the space pointing to the Vernal Equinox. And now, following the Piscean Age, it is the sign of Aquarius that will next point to the Vernal Equinox. This brings in the new age that we are anticipating.

Each sign of the Zodiac occupies thirty degrees of the astrological circle which covers a period of time of approximately 2,000 years. Each of these periods of time of 2,000 years or more is called a month of the Great Year. These periods are also called Platonic or Solar Years.

This makes us realize that the last Aquarian Age was somewhat more than 25,000 years ago. It was during this ancient time that artists painted their extraordinary visions on the walls of caves at Lascaux in France and at Altamira in Spain. These paintings reflect a remarkable level of sophistication and insight.

From the coming Aquarian Age will emerge many new realities and energies. More people will realize the need to be in touch with the inner world. As we understand ourselves, we will understand more clearly other peoples of the world and thereby enter into a more evolved and whole consciousness. The mystic, Nicholas of Cusa, had God say: "Know thyself and I shall be thine."

THE GREAT YEAR
Chapter Two

It takes the axis of the earth approximately 25,920 terrestial years to move full circle from the vernal point in the Zodiacal circle to its starting point again, so that a Great New Year begins. There are approximately two thousand terrestial years in one Great Month. Twelve Great Months, one for each sign of the Zodiac, make a Great Year or a Cosmic Year.

Some Great Months are longer than 2,000 terrestial years, depending on how extended the constellation of that sign is in the sky. Pisces is an extended constellation, so that the Piscean Great Month, that is the Piscean Age, is longer than 2,000 years.

From the sun and planets, the earth receives influence which is filtered through the signs of the Zodiac. In response to this influence, civilization on earth is transformed; ideas in religion, science, and the arts change perceptibly as each sign of the Zodiac moves into its place approximately every two thousand years. Patterns of life and the archetypes which inform them undergo alteration in response to the radiation of the particular constellation in which the vernal point is moving throughout the more than 2,000 years that a Great Month lasts. Therefore, as each new Great Month is experienced, humanity moves toward the achievement of a new kind of consciousness. In other words, each age brings humankind to a new stage of evolution.

Despite this evolutionary thrust of chronological time, there is often a sudden decline after a great civilization has been achieved. The highly developed "fathers" of a nation are often followed by degenerate and weak-willed descendants. A nation that was once powerful can fall into disrepute, leaving only the dross of its best ideas and creations. Even so, there are always some people who resist such collective disintegration and relate to new patterns or archetypes in a creative, forward-moving way. These people soften the birth pangs of a new age, refusing to be caught in fear of the unknown or slowed by the roadblocks which others throw in the path of creative change.

Our present time illustrates the ways in which these forces of regression and evolution encounter each other. This period preceding the new cosmic month of Aquarius is one of chaos, crime, and terrorism. Institutions fulfill limited individualist needs, and collective structures, often managed by egocentric and tyrant-like leaders, keep old values alive. Under such systems, only a few people benefit while the majority suffers. Thus, the meaning and fulfillment of the new cosmic year are in jeopardy.

Now let us examine closely the chart of a Great Year and the ways in which the twelve Great Months contribute to the evolution of humankind. If you refer to the chart in the back of the book, you will see that each circle represents approximately two thousand years. Our knowledge of each age is exceedingly limited for the reason that, until the beginning of the Taurian Age, approximately 4,000 BCE, there were no written records.

Nevertheless, we know something of the Cancerian Age, that of cardinal water, through stories and myths that have come to us through the oral tradition. Countries all over the world have in common ancient stories of floods and deluges, allowing us to assume that such natural disasters involving water occurred during the Cancerian Age. It has been suggested that Atlantis, with its fabled civilization, sank below the waters of the Mediterranean Sea during this era. Myriads of ships from times long past are known to be sunk in the harbors of Crete.

We also know something about the Geminian Age, a mutable sign with the twins as symbol, represented by Castor and Pollux, the Dioscuri of Zeus. In Hebrew Scriptures we read about Jacob and Esau, the twin sons of Isaac and Rebecca. Another pair of twins is Romulus and Remus who are considered the founders of the great city of Rome. It is hard to determine the dates of any of these stories, so we must be content to categorize them as simply "ancient."

The Taurean Age covered the period of time between 4,000 and 2,000 BCE. This Great Month brought to fantastic heights the civilization of Egypt, the island of Crete, and Mycenae and Tiryns on the mainland of Greece. Records of these cultures have been left in the pyramids, the Sphinx, the tombs, and in papyrus scrolls dating around 4,000 BCE, and were found also in cuneiform on clay tablets. Remains of the ancient Egyptian civilization reveal much use of the elements of that Taurean Age—earth and water.

Taurus is a feminine, fixed[1], earth sign ruled by Venus. The symbol of this sign is the Bull, the glyph ♉ representing the bull's head and horns. Coming in the spring of the year, this sign stands for the blossoming time in plant life.

In ascertaining the meaning of a Zodiacal sign as it defines a particular Great Month, we need also to look at the sign directly opposite. The Zodiac sign that names the age always falls in the first house of the chart. The opposite House is always the seventh house and gives an effect which is less personal as well as wider in

1. Fixed signs are resistant to change. Fixity relates to stability, steadfastness, but lack of volatility. They are known as cornerstones of support. They may not start anything but will guard and preserve what is started. Their faults are inertia and lack of imagination. Taurus and Scorpio, Leo and Aquarius are Fixed Quadruplicity.

scope. The two signs constellate a polarity, just as the North Pole does with the South Pole. The principle of one sign can complement its opposite but there can also be tensions between the two signs.

For Taurus the opposite sign is Scorpio, a feminine, fixed, water sign ruled by Mars and Pluto, who make for great intensity. Unlike any other, the sign of Scorpio, with the glyph ♏, has two symbols: the scorpion that bites its own tail and the eagle which can reach great heights. The two dimensions reflected in this sign—the earthy scorpion and the soaring eagle—make it clearly a symbol of death and rebirth.

As an earth sign, Taurus is always concerned with concrete reality. What better manifestation of the Taurean Age, then, than the magnificent pyramids, the only one of the seven wonders of the ancient world that is still in complete form. The occupations of the people of this age were agriculture and cattle raising. With the water of the Nile giving them ample opportunity to become agriculturists and gardeners, they were amazingly related to and proficient in growing food for themselves and their cattle.

The early Egyptians were deeply related to the myth of death and resurrection (a characteristic of Scorpio), as shown by the stability of their underground tombs which contained all the belongings of the dead. Even food was left in tombs to carry the deceased through to the other

side of life. This was the civilization that
prepared for the Night Sea Journey, a ritual
relating to the sun's disappearance in the west
each night and its emergence in the east each
morning. Each night a solar boat was made
ready to follow its course through the watery
deeps where it suffered death before it was
reborn each morning.

The agrarian Taurean culture was depen-
dent on the phases of the moon with its dark and
light periods. Again we can see how the principle
of death-rebirth was emphasized, how the feminine earth sign of Taurus complemented the
Scorpio water sign. In the larger-than-life carvings on the great columns of the temple at Luxor,
nature symbols abound. There one can see large,
finely sculpted bees, a symbol of the goddess
Venus, who is also ruler of Taurus. A deeply
honored part of the Egyptian civilization, the
feminine was expressed in the form of many goddesses whose officiants were often female.

Egypt's savior-god, Osiris, was worshipped
in bull form as the Apis Bull. He was slain each
year as an atonement for the sins of the people. In
the rebirth ceremony, Isis, his wife, was represented as the Golden Cow. By gathering the scattered parts of Osiris' body and reuniting them,
Isis made it possible for him to be resurrected
after every sacrifice. The Apis Bull was honored
with its own burial tomb. A crescent moon, symbol of the feminine principle, was on the bull's

forehead. When a sacred Apis Bull died, or was ritually slain, he was not replaced until another bull with the crescent moon on its forehead could be found. When ritually slain by the priest, the bull was considered an ever-dying and ever-resurrected god. On the island of Crete can be found many expressions of the bull athletes or bull dancers, reminding us of these ancient religious rites.

The elements of earth and water, the qualities of Taurus and its opposite, Scorpio, fashioned this age in a very particular way. It was the combination of the sandy earth and the vast Nile River, with its rich alluvial soil which overflowed each year, that made the Nile Valley seem like a green river flowing on either side of the blue river, from the southern end of Egypt to the Mediterranean Sea in the north. Over the centuries, this valley has been the source of food for surrounding lands, reminding us that both the Taurean Age and Taurean people are especially related to growing things.

For many generations, the Israelites, offspring of Joseph, lived in Egypt as bonded servants. Their main occupation was to build the pyramids. Here we encounter the mixture of myth and history—the book of Exodus is the source of this material. At one time, the Pharaoh seemed ready to release them from their slavery, but at the last minute his heart was hardened. Finally God visited a plague upon the Egyptians, who, in their anger at the disaster, would not let the Israelites go. Ten times the Pharaoh was ready to release the Israelites, and ten times God, in his ambivalence, hardened Pharaoh's heart, thus stopping the exodus of the Israelites from Egypt.

Then God said to Moses that the firstborn Egyptian males of humans and animals would be killed. Only the firstborn of the Israelites would be spared, and then only if the blood of a sacrificed lamb were placed on the lintel of each door, to let the angel of death know to spare that home. While death passed over the dwellings of the Israelites, all Egyptians suffered the loss of their firstborn males. In his grief over losing his firstborn son, Pharaoh relented and let the Israelites go.

At the last minute, however, the Egyptians rushed after the Israelites, pursuing them on foot and in horse-drawn chariots to the edge of the Red Sea which God had parted for his oppressed people. The water rose over the Egyptians and they were drowned in the watery mud of their own land. One could say that the mighty Pyramids in existence today, six thousand years later, and the continuing productivity of the Nile Valley are evidence that the symbols of the age—earth and water—found fulfillment in the Egyptian civilization. However, these same symbols, or elements, were what destroyed the Egyptian people and their power. By resisting change, the Egyptians failed to use their symbols for transformation and the fulfillment of their great civilization.

As the Egyptians were drowning in the Red Sea, it must be remembered that the Israelites were following a pillar of cloud by day and a pillar of fire by night as they moved toward the land that promised to bring them fulfillment. These elements of fire and air take us to the Arien Age which is the next "new footstep of God" and which follows the end of the Taurean Age.

The Arien Age covers the 2,000-year period of the Hebrew Scriptures as well as the developing Greek culture. The last five hundred years of this age was the time of great flowering for Greece, which continued to flourish through the first five hundred years of CE of the Piscean Age.

Aries, as a cardinal[1] fire sign, is an initiatory, masculine sign ruled by Mars. The symbol for this age is the Ram which shows in the glyph ♈ as the ram's horn. The sign opposite it on the chart is Libra, also a cardinal sign. Libra is an air sign ruled by Venus, and its symbol is the scale, suggesting balance and, more specifically, justice. The glyph for Libra is ♎ and is a graphic representation of balance. Both elements here, fire and air, are masculine

---

1. Cardinal signs. Outgoing. Each in its own way takes definite action. People with these signs set things going, are leaders, and work to an end. Their faults may be restlessness. Aries and Leo, Cancer and Capricorn make the Cardinal Quadruplicity.

elements. Although Venus, as the ruler of Libra, brought a feminine aspect, there was a definite change toward the masculine during this age.

Fire, the element of this new great month, the Arien Age, is an element of great destruction or great transformation. It represent passion, intensity, vitality, and will. The Hebrew Scriptures begin with the consistent use of the symbols of this age. We see Moses, the monumental man of this fire age, led to the burning bush where he communicates with the monotheistic God, "I am that I am," on Mount Horeb. The burning bush and the pillar of fire show the way for Moses who, although he was found in the bullrushes by the Pharaoh's daughter and was reared as an Egyptian prince, led the Israelites out of the spiritual darkness prevailing in Egypt at that time. This physical exodus of the Israelites from Egypt to the Promised Land, from bondage to freedom, coincides with the move from the Taurean Age into the pioneering, initiatory, Arien Age. Just as the Israelites had difficulty breaking from the Egyptians, so did the Arien Age struggle to free itself from the goddess-dominated mystery religions and to worship, instead, one patriarchal God.

When the Israelites suffered alienation from God, they were able to establish relationship again by repenting and offering a lamb as burnt sacrifice. The Ten Commandments became the first written code of conduct, reflecting the value of justice and the influence of Libra, the sign opposite to Aries. It was during this period that Hammurabi encouraged the writing of the sacred code of conduct, also the result of Librian influence.

After the flight from Egypt, the children of Israel expected matters to move easily and quickly for them. In part, their expectations were met. But often their trusted leader, Moses, had to leave them to speak with God about where next to lead the people. After one of these absences, Moses returned to find the people worshipping the Golden Calf, or regressing to the past age and its devotion to the goddesses. The Israelites were severely punished for their disobedience, and many were killed. Even so, they persisted for nearly four thousand years in their covert and forbidden worshipping of various goddesses, and each time they were punished. Finally, goddess worship— and with it, an honoring of the feminine—was eliminated. Only during the last few decades of the Piscean Age has the goddess emerged again and been creatively included in the spiritual lives of humankind.

When Moses left his people, presumably to go to heaven, they were lost without his shepherding. They longed for a figure that could lead them to safe places. Over and over, the Psalms express this. Likewise, the prophets, bringing the word of God to the Israelites again and again, struggled to keep them loyal to Yahweh rather than allowing them to fall into alienated and heathen ways. Like Noah, the Israelites of this period needed a covenant with God to help them remain faithful to his commandments. The concept of a messiah arose out of this need for leadership and shepherding and evolved into the image of a "coming one." Isaiah spoke of one whose work would lead the Israelites to salvation, redeeming them from personal sin and political oppression. Thus, the people grew to think of the messiah as both a spiritual and political savior, as one who would remove them from the dominance of Rome and establish a theocracy.

Though many outstanding individuals arose as kings or prophets, and several of them emphasized the need for justice, none fulfilled the role of the messiah who was to shepherd the people in a fatherly, protective way. So the Arien Age ended for the people of Israel without an individual coming forward as a leading figure. Except in isolated situations—the prophets and some of the kings—the element of fire did not take the Israelites far enough toward being individuals. Most of the people remained tribal, relying on the great ram's horn, the shofar, to call them to worship and to battle.

More individuality was developed by the educated Greeks, whose civilization emerged during the last five hundred years of the Arien Age. They took intellectual initiative and expressed spiritual concerns, suggesting the influence of the cardinal, pioneering sign of Aries.

In the ram's horn, carried on the Greek helmets worn by soldiers, can be seen a symbol of the age. A new awareness for the activity of Mars, the ruler of Aries, showed in the concern of the Greeks for sports and in the beginning of competitive games.

Between 650 and 550 BCE, four great world teachers were born: Buddha, Confucius, Lao Tsu, and Zoroaster. They brought new understanding, new depth to the realm of the spirit. About seven years before the beginning of the Piscean Age is possibly the time Jesus of Nazareth was born, adding to the list of spiritual leaders that came into the world during the last part of the Arien Age.

A large star, made up of the conjunction of Saturn and Jupiter, happened three times near the end of May, in 7 BCE. Jung, who speaks of this in *Aion*, favors a late date in May of that year as the time Jesus was born. Ancient knowledge says that the sign of the "twins," referring to the sign of Gemini which falls at the end of May, carries within itself the two halves of the Tree of the Knowledge of Good and Evil. It is apparent in the records of Jesus' life that he struggled to integrate these two opposites in his life time.

The Tree of the Knowledge of Good and Evil and the Tree of Life were the two trees in the center of the Garden of Eden. This myth, as does all myth, represents what takes place in our psyches. It is inside ourselves that we find the meaning. If we can see the Garden of Eden as an unconscious manifestation of the Self, then the Tree of the Knowledge of Good and Evil is rooted in our inner being. Similarly, the Tree of Life, also mentioned in the myth, is rooted in our inner being. As the myth in Genesis implies, these two trees are *a priori* at the center of each of us. It must be emphasized that this myth is an inner reality rather than an outer one; myth tells the reality of what is found in our psyches, and what happens in our inner world.

With the Tree of the Knowledge of Good and Evil at the center of our being, put there by the God of gods, how can we say we do not have evil in us as well as good? The Tree of Life remains to have its fruit eaten when we become conscious enough to return to the Garden of Eden, past the cherubim with the flaming swords that guard the entrance! In the light of this understanding, Jesus' integration of the opposites of good and evil gives evidence of a spiritual maturity most unusual for his time or for any time.

Although the Arien Age ended with the release of some great spiritual forces, as illustrated in the lives of Jesus and other great world teachers, few people mastered the fiery elements that can lead to wholeness and individuation. The Israelites still looked for someone who would remove from them their sin and guilt; they believed another would bring salvation, a messiah who would come and restore their country to a theocracy.

The old Great Year ended with the Arien Age, and with Pisces a new Great Year began. The Arien people had to go on and slowly realize that the ark of the covenant had lost the intensity of its spiritual power and that there was no leader to reclaim it for them. Though this fire age, with its great potency, ended without the realization of the Jews' desire for a messiah, five spiritual leaders had been born to bring a new eminence to the planet. Jesus was born so near the Piscean Age that influence from him was carried over into the development of Christianity, which occurred as a result of his disciples' efforts rather than any of his own. The disciples brought as much of the teaching of Jesus as they had absorbed but it was far from all he was teaching.

After the death of Jesus and the post-crucifixion events, the disciples went into the Mediterranean world with the message that Jesus would come a second time since he had already risen once. They also took with them the message that Jesus could forgive sins and redeem the souls of those who believed in him. Furthermore, they said, life was eternal. With this message of love and light, Christianity was born, taking root as an underground activity in pagan Rome. By the third century CE, it was well established in the Mediterranean world, offering an alternative—indeed standing as a contradiction—to the darkness of the mystery religions that existed at that time. Although there was much truth and earthy value surrounding these unknown mystery religions, there were also practices of human sacrifice and healing not understood by people excluded from such rituals.

In the next chapter we will move to material about the Piscean Age, which is the age of Christianity. Except as it relates to the patterns of the Piscean Age, however, Christianity will not be the focus of the discussion.

THE FIRST MONTH OF A GREAT NEW YEAR:

THE PISCEAN AGE

Chapter Three

All of us alive today have lived in the first month of the Great New Year, also called the Cosmic Year. This first month, known as the Piscean Age, covers approximately two thousand years, beginning about sixty years before the first century and extending beyond the year 2000. It is an age of tremendous change. For example, many people born in the first decade of this twentieth century have known what it is like to travel by horse and buggy, automobile, and jet planes—by steam, oil, and solar energy. The last thirty years especially suggest that the momentum of change has speeded up, with every moment bringing something new into the material world. Dramatic spiritual changes have also taken place during this time, although their nature is such that we cannot measure or even name them as yet.

The horoscope for an age, as well as for an individual, is divided into twelve houses, each house representing some facet of life. In any discussion of the horoscope of an age, as in this

chapter, statements about each house suggest
the collective attitudes of the people as well as
ways in which individual persons might best respond to the givens of their time. But the horoscope of an age speaks in generalities about these
various parts of life, as reflected in the twelve
houses, and is in no way as specific as the chart
of an individual. An individual chart, for example, may show some houses with one or more
planets in them, making the personal horoscope
more complex and particular than that of an age.
On the other hand, the planet that rules a certain
sign of the Zodiac is constant; Aries is always ruled by Mars, Taurus by Venus, Gemini by Mercury, and so on. (See the chart inserted in this
book.) We must remember that the ruling planet
of the sign adds greatly to its meaning.

Let us look at the sign of Pisces. It is a mutable[1] water sign— the symbol of two fishes tied together going in opposite directions—and is ruled
by Jupiter and Neptune. Being a feminine sign,
Pisces takes in spirit, associated more with masculine signs, through matter and the body. This
unity of spirit/matter in the Piscean Age has been
broken, however, when the fire of life, or the driving force of Pisces, has not been able to keep the

1. Mutable signs. Adaptable. They have a tendency to
change or inconsistency. They are also called Common,
meaning serving together. Their faults are over-diffusive-
ness and lack of stability. Gemini and Sagittarius, Virgo and
Pisces are the Mutable Quadruplicity.

opposites together. We have only to think of the many people of this age who have suffered from a spirit/mind/body split to find examples of how our original oneness has been disrupted. The integration of opposites, which comes with wholeness, has been difficult to achieve and maintain, although many individuals of this time have accomplished it.

The two fishes of Pisces represent a person's dual nature, that which is visible to the outer world and that reality which is hidden within. In the symbol of the two fishes, the glyph X shows this duality. Like every mutable sign, Pisces is flexible, open to change, adapting to circumstances rather easily. This quality of mutability, along with the element of water and its instability, makes Pisces the most fluid of all signs. On the negative side, the quality of withdrawnness is more marked in Pisces than in other signs.

As suggested above, the Piscean symbol of the two fishes going in opposite directions would indicate a splitting of the opposites. However, the double pull on the Piscean person does not necessarily result in division, for Jupiter, as one ruler of Pisces, brings an expansive attitude toward life. This allows many possibilities within, including that of integration, to emerge and unfold.

The fishes dwell in the expanse and depth of the ocean. Although they can come to the surface of consciousness, they mostly live in the greater depths of the unconscious where the roots of feelings, thoughts, and deeds originate. Even though the people of this era, the Piscean Age, have been aware of themselves as individuals rather than as part of a tribe, as in the Arien Age, still they have so identified with the unconscious that, except in rare cases, there has been little conscious relationship to the inner world. The result of this identification with the unconscious is that the irrational side of human nature has been easily ignored, put down, or covered up.

As stated before, when one considers the qualities of any sign, the opposite Zodiacal sign is important to contemplate. This is particularly true of the sign for an age. The sign opposite Pisces is Virgo, a mutable earth sign whose symbol is the Virgin. The earth signs are practical and more withdrawn, but when combined with mutability, as carried by Virgo in this case, they can be more free. We remember that all earth and water signs are feminine and are known as negative signs. Astrologically this means that they repress themselves while being receptive, and in this way are different from fire and air, which are more outgoing and self-expressing, and are known as masculine, positive signs.

Virgo is a sign of service and of the harvest, making it a fertility sign. Often the Virgin is pictured not only with the child but also with an ear of corn. While the Virgin herself gives the feeling of purity and chastity, the potential of nurturing motherhood is seen in the grain she holds and in the child. Thus, the Virgin brings the harvest as one brings the fruit of one's labors into being, for the myth of the virginal birth is an important inner reality, involving the birth of the Divine Child or Self within.

It is in the depths of the soul that this Divine Child or Self is born and grows, engaging one in a life's work which Jung speaks of as the indivuation process. New life comes from that virginal part within us which is unknown, unused, which is waiting for the spirit to infuse and fulfill it. The birth for us can be a new insight that changes our attitudes, a new artistic gift, or perhaps a dream of the Divine Child, which can indicate the Self coming to birth within us. Again, as with all myth, the Virgin Birth stories found in various traditions speak of an inner reality rather than of outer, historical events.

Despite the limitations of the Piscean Age, a greater number of people have functioned as individuals in this time than in former millennia. One needs only to remember a few names—St. Augustine, Mohammed, St. Theresa—and imagine the lives of many nameless but whole men and women in order to realize the possiblility of individuation in this time.

From the beginning, this has been an unsettled and unsettling age. The shepherd, or the messiah, whom the Arien Age Israelites had hoped would emerge to lead the people, did not materialize. The end of the Arien Age was not unlike the ending of this Piscean Age, except that the unrest of the present time is greater and more complex because of the billions of people covering the planet today.

At this juncture of Arien and Piscean ages, between the seemingly irreconcilable opposites of Fire and Water, Jesus of Nazareth was born. We can surmise that his being unfolded with intensity and growth of consciousness as he lived and taught in the first part of the first century, CE. His life, lived so totally in dialogue with God, showed an amazing level of consciousness, ending with his crucifixion after relatively few years. Through Jesus' relationship to the Source, he lived his own myth. He lived what he taught to such an extent that he had become the paradigm of the mature person, the Aquarian man of 2000 years later. More about this will be said in Chapter Five.

Through the experience of the apostles and the work of Paul, Christianity slowly developed to become the new religion. By establishing relatedness to the divine through baptism by water, Christianity brought an end to the burnt animal sacrifices of the Arien Age. Instead of animals it became the human who was offered to God; instead of fire, the element of transformation and worship became water.

Jesus, as the Christ, was worshipped as God, becoming the object of devotion and a model for the religious way. He symbolized everything that was bright, loving and on the side of good. The belief in the divinity of Jesus Christ offered humanity forgiveness of sin, salvation, and life everlasting.

One must understand how much of the darkness of the previous times, under the pantheon of Greek and Roman gods, still gripped the people. Their imaginations were not free from the images of many-faceted gods who embodied reckless passion, dark unknowns, slavery, human sacrifice, and constant dalliance with mortals on earth. The world of the Mediterranean longed for more religious security and found it in the light, bright, loving Jesus Christ who promised life everlasting as well as sprritual safety.

Not only was the struggle between pagan darkness and Christian light a difficult and serious one, but there was dissonance between the God of the Hebrews, who proclaimed, "I create good and I create evil," who inspired fear, awe, respect, and reverence, and Jesus Christ, who was the symbol of complete love and acceptance. Clearly some new and vital religious consciousness was being born during this juncture of ages.

Because the sign of the fishes belongs to the water triplicity, one of the three water signs of the Zodiac, the Piscean Age has required that humanity stand up to the challenge of water by conquering and transforming it. This was the age of exploring the great oceans and seas that cover the face of the earth. Oarsmen, whose rhythmic beat carried slight wooden shells over the seas to land on unknown shores, were the first to begin this exploration. Later, sails were launched on large ships, allowing the wind to carry humans across great expanses of water. Mastery of the sea brought gold from the Americas to fill the coffers of European countries. Spices and exotic materials were brought from the Orient to Europe where markets were eager to learn about preserving food with spices and to enjoy the rich silks from the Orient.

Great cities grew along rivers large enough to accommodate ocean-going vessels, linking the four corners of the earth. River and ocean traffic encouraged the birth and growth of industry, so that tilling the soil, planting, and herding animals ceased to be the main work of humankind.

As time moved toward the second millennium, people passed the test of conquering the element of water by changing its quality. Treated with intense heat, water was turned to steam, a new energy force. With the steamship it became possible to make larger ships that could take longer voyages, across every ocean, and discovver more new land. Many people began to recognize the world as larger than expected.

As the use of steam energy increased, the industrial growth of countries increased; towns and cities grew in size with people moving closer together, establishing neighborhoods, shaping

each other through social customs, economic ex-
changes, and religious practices. With the transformation of water into steam, the test of the Piscean Age was met and the urban style of life was
born.

The three water signs, Pisces, Cancer, and
Scorpio, are known to have a flow and rhythm
that encourage artistic expression. The Piscean
Age has excelled in the expansion of art: Gothic
cathedrals, great literature, magnificent painting
and sculpture, rich music. Again the names go
on and on: Dante, Chaucer, Shakespeare, Mil-
ton, Michelangelo, Leonardo da Vinci, Rembrandt,
Van Gogh, Bach, Mozart, Beethoven, Schubert, to
name a very few of those people who left a legacy
of beauty over the last thousand years of the
Piscean era. One is struck by the sheer amount
of fine art from this period. It is interesting
to note how religious subjects have been central
to the content of art; devoted people working
under Piscean influence have produced inspiring
results.

Outside the monasteries, where knowledge
was kept alive, illiteracy prevailed in the Middle
Ages. As a consequence, the cathedral was the
book of the people as well as the house of God. In
the bas-reliefs inside and outside the cathedrals
one can see stories told in carvings of the Hebrew
Scriptures, teaching people through images
about Bible characters and their lives. On cathedral walls, one can also see the Zodiacal signs

carved in stone, for astrology was part of every day life; scholars as well as the uneducated knew astrology to be heart knowledge, to be felt rather than analyzed logically. In Chartres Cathedral, to give only one example, the walls have bas-reliefs of the symbols of the Zodiac and the planets. Next to those are the carvings of the activities of that period of the year. February, for example, might show the Aquarian symbol and a man huddled around a fireplace doing some handicraft; or September might show Virgo in the midst of rich harvesting scenes. In this way, the calendar emerged.

Although most churches profess a great rejection of astrology, today the four fixed signs of the Zodiac, representing the four evangelists, are found in many ancient and modern churches. Luke is represented by the Taurian Bull; Mark by the Lion of Leo; John by the Scorpion/Eagle; and Matthew by the Aquarian person.

Although this ancient wisdom of astrology dominated the thinking of the Middle Ages, it became taboo at the time of the Renaissance. Humankind began to study itself to a greater extent, and as the age of science began, it meant acausal systems of knowledge were suspect and of the devil. As one of the greatest tools in helping individuals relate to the archetypal patterning of their psyches, astrology was denied any real field of activity until the late nineteenth century when it slowly was revived again largely by the astrologer Allen Leo.

Now let us look more specifically at the chart of the Piscean Age, touching on each of the twelve houses, but emphasizing those which have shaped this age in significant ways.

The *First House* has the sign of Pisces, which is ruled by the planets Jupiter and Neptune. This indicates the general qualities of the people living under the sign. Piscean people are the most sensitive of the water signs, sacrificing for others, tending toward selflessness. As water needs a container to have shape, so do Pisceans need form, shaping themselves by models given by others. Since the life and words of Jesus made him an object of devotion, Christianity became the form, the model for many people of this age. For others it has been the Hebrew religion or Islam or Oriental religions. The particular forms of Christianity, Judaism, and Islam emerged and polarized during this age even though all three religions share the same oral tradition, the same God, the same holy city, Jerusalem, and much that is in the Hebrew Scriptures.

Another characteristic of Piscean people is that they are usually able to give imagination and intuition concrete expression. Neptunian inspiration is behind the work of many artists, particularly that of Michelangelo. Although impressions from the inner world come easily and are given artistic life, Pisceans nevertheless find it difficult to relate to the unconscious because they are often so completely identified with it. Just as water represents the unconscious, so are Pisceans, people of a water sign, identified with the unconscious. To relate to the unconscious requires separation from it which is what Pisceans generally cannot achieve. They get messages of inspiration or imagination through dreams, visions, or from empathetic responses to another person but seldom from conscious work. Their feeling of self is often surrendered, making them seem muddled, up in the air, without attainable hopes.

Jupiter brings a sense of justice and compassion to the Piscean character but can also kindle sentimentality, seen especially in the romance novels of the last two hundred years. Finally, Pisceans are literal people; things must be carried out in fact, rather than in symbol or in attitude as is beginning to happen now.

The *Second House* has to do with our relation to financial matters, possessions, and feelings. During this period of Christianity, which covers the Piscean Age, the sign of Aries, ruled by the planet Mars, is in this Second House. Known as the god of war, Mars has contributed to competitiveness in business and acquisitiveness of money and objects, resulting in their inflated importance and value. Feelings have been more repressed than expressed, especially under the influence of Christianity which discourages negative thoughts and their articulation. Christianity sees evil as the absence of good rather than as something in itself; acknowledgment of personal darkness has not been allowed until very recently.

The *Third House* indicates the quality of mental activity, communication, and one's environment, which includes brothers and sisters and others close to a person besides the parents. Here we find Taurus ruled by Venus, whose influence can be seen in the romantic and sometimes sentimental feelings and attitudes of this period, expressed especially in poetic writing and novels of the last few hundred years. However, we must remember that true feeling in relationship has been repressed consistently.

During the Middle Ages there was little communicating among people except as they spoke between themselves in dialogue. Outside of the monasteries most people could neither read nor write and, therefore, had little to stimulate them mentally beyond live human interaction. Before the printing press was invented, knowledge was of a practical nature and was exchanged in the process of work or play. The imaginative Piscean mentality generated and kept alive many folktales, passing them on from generation to generation through story telling, drama, and the visual arts. At holiday times, the occasions of entertainment were mystery and miracle plays, performed in churches, courtyards, and town squares.

Adding to the ease and frequency of communication in the Piscean Age has been the air travel of this last century. The conquering of outer space has also led to a phenomenal increase in travel and communication, anticipating the Aquarian air age. It makes one wonder how travel and communication will change in the twenty-first century.

The *Fourth House* relates to our attitudes toward what surrounds and protects. This is principally the home, particularly the early home, but it can also be the womb and the tomb. The home of childhood is where foundations are laid and first wounds are frequently inflicted. With Gemini here ruled by Mercury, there is an emphasis on thinking rather than feeling. Gemini is a double sign—the Twins—which can indicate a one-sided approach to things or a black and white attitude that does not try to find the third point, the point of integration. This split attitude has been most visible in this last age. Because change is important to Gemini people, and doing rather than being is often favored by them, the rootedness that is soul fulfilling may be absent.

The fields of interest in the *Fifth House* include the god Eros, who rules love affairs, children, creativity, artistic expression, and all pleasures. Here the sign of Cancer, ruled by the Moon, lends its nurturing, mothering, feeling influence, particularly in the area of parenting. However, out of too much self-sacrificing and the desire for something in return, can come self-centeredness and possessiveness. Again we see how poetry, music, drama, and art have flourished during this age, with romance recurring as a major theme. Suffering has been regarded as punishment, not as a way to grow, with happiness (or the illusion of happiness) named as the reason for being.

The *Sixth House* of daily work and health has the sign of Leo, ruled by the Sun. Because of its luminosity and strength, the sun indicates what is the most important form of self-expression. It seems that in the Piscean Age, one's work is valued most. As if knowing another's occupation will bring true relatedness, one quickly asks a new acquaintance, "What is your line of work?" We are more content with ourselves when we are settled in work we like, perhaps because work gives us a greater sense of identity than that which comes with play, friendship, or even family. Too frequently, work becomes so important that it dominates one's life, leaving one an ambitious workaholic, driving one to be ahead, if not first, in the chosen profession. More than other aspects of life, our professions determine the social, political, and economic class in which we find ourselves. It is no surprise, then, that those who are competitive by nature most likely give their energies to rivalries in the workplace rather than to relationships or play.

Because the Sun rules the sixth house and

also because of the general compassion of Pisces, health has been an object of interest and concern to the people. The highly rational approach to health and medicine, resulting in much research and experimentation as well as an explosion of knowledge, has been fostered by the patriarchal ambiance dominating the Piscean Age. Millions of lives have been saved through improved surgical procedures and inoculation for diseases; antibiotics have kept many illnesses from being the killers they have been in the past. Increased knowledge about every part of the body has caused doctors to specialize, so that every organ now seems to need a specialist. During this age, the medical doctor has become the most revered among professionals, serving people in small towns as confidante and counselor as well as healer. It is wonderful to see women doctors growing in number; the "he" profession is changing to be also a "she" profession as new patterning is felt from the approaching Aquarian Age.

Water, the element of this age, changed medical sciences when its healing properties were acknowledged. Spas, medicinal baths, salt water baths, hot and cold compresses show the use of water in the curing of many ills. Indeed, this has been a very curing time.

Virgo, ruled by Mercury, the opposite sign of Pisces, falls in the *Seventh House*, that which speaks of the other in marriage and partnerships.

During the Christian era, the virgin has been considered the ideal marriage partner. The virginal quality of Virgo can be seen in the vow of chastity required of each person wishing to enter a religious order. Virgo also gives service. The down-to-earth help we offer to each other is what allows organizations, communities, or homes to run in a practical, smooth way. Of course, this ideal of service is not always embodied in partnerships and communities.

Virgo and Mercury, its ruler, bring a rational approach to life. This combination could account for the marriages that have been arranged for practical, reasonable considerations.

The *Eighth House* holds the sign of Libra ruled by Venus. Dealing with possessions as inheritances that are gained through others and the feelings that are involved, it has to do also with sacrifice. This house is a bridge to the next one of religion. In the eighth house is indicated what must be sacrificed to reach the next house of religion. Christianity is thought of as the religion of love, but Venus is sacrificed, so love and the feminine qualities are in the unconscious. That is, love is not as available to Piscean people as a whole, unless one is aware of the lack and consciously struggles to redeem it. We must know that an ego conscious of the missing quality can work to bring about the expression of it.

When we reach the house of religion, we realize that the sacrifice of Venus left Mars totally unrelated to love and the feminine. Unhindered, Mars could do his work, dark as it has been. The sacrifice of Venus in the Eighth House could be one of the reasons that feelings, especially negative ones, have not been expressed very adequately.

We see the *Ninth House*, the house of religion, under the sign of Scorpio ruled by the planets Mars and Pluto. Scorpio is the only sign that has two symbols to represent it, as has been said above. One is the scorpion that bites its own tail, indicating the depth of degradation and lack of self-love that is possible for Scorpio. The other symbol is the eagle, soaring to great heights, showing that it is possible for this sign to be related to higher values.

One negative of this era comes from the proselytizing of Christian leaders. By forcing upon primitive tribes a foreign and incomprehensible religion, Christian missionaries took from natives the basic nourishment of their spiritual life. Another negative is found in the chronic religious oppression characterizing this age—the persecution of the Christians by the Romans, of the Jews by the Christians, of Christians by Christians, of Arabs by Jews or Jews by Arabs. The warlikeness and hostility of Mars shows most specifically in the Christian Crusades, in the Spanish Inquisition, and in every war given to settling boundaries in the Christian world. We cannot forget the two world wars, periods of much violence and turmoil, that took place in this last century. Nor can we overlook the wars which have occurred on our own continent, from the warlike Aztecs forcing the Toltecs to change their peaceful ways to the slaughter taking place now in Nicaragua, Guatemala, and Chile. The god of war and aggression has dominated this house of religion that spoke of love as its fundamental premise but brought much bloodshed.

We must remember that Pluto also is a ruler of Scorpio. First seen in 1930, this small planet is the furthest planet from the Sun. Fifteen years after the discovery of Pluto, before we hardly knew the power of plutonium, the first bomb was dropped on Hiroshima, August 6, 1945.

Pluto is the god of the unconscious. If not related to, the unconscious can be frightening in its collective power. As mentioned before, the Piscean Age has not been able to know much about the unconscious and so has suffered from tremendous fear. As we move into the Aquarian Age, having acquired more knowledge of the unconscious through what has been learned from depth psychology, literature, and art, we are strengthening our relationship to the inner world. Pluto wants change. If it does not occur naturally, change may come violently. If creative change is welcomed and implemented, it can be a transforming event.

Fire, that element so favorable to the Arien

Age and its dialogue with God through burnt of-
ferings, has been used religiously in the Piscean
Age for punishment and destruction. Jeanne
d'Arc, Savonarola and many others condemned
for witchcraft were burned at the stake to destroy
the "demons" believed to be inside them.

At the beginning of the Piscean era, John the
Baptist was preaching that people must bring
forth fruits worthy of repentance, saying that the
threshing floor is to be cleared, the wheat will be
gathered into the garner but the chaff will be
burned with an unquenchable fire. Again we see
that the element of one age becomes negative if
used in the next. The fire of Aries is negative in the
Piscean age of water.

The *Tenth House* emphasizes the outer world
and professions, and is under the sign of
Sagittarius with Jupiter ruling. This sign with its
ruler has a more religious connotation than any
other sign in the Zodiac. Jupiter can bring good
and the expanding sense of self into the outer
world. On the other hand, under other circumstances, the expansion can portend an inflated attitude.

The sign here points to the importance of
what one does professionally, just as the Sixth
House emphasizes our daily work. If an inflation-
ary feeling enters in, a god-like attitude might
even be present. Here in the Tenth House one
finds one's place in the world. Christianity felt its
message should be carried to all areas in the

world. To many missionaries, finding a "place in the world" meant imposing their Christian beliefs on the more primitive people of the earth. Using religious vocation as their justification, many Christians exploited American Indians on this continent, behaving similarly in Asia, Africa, and other remote parts of the world.

The *Eleventh House* is related to friendships and to social activities and organizations. Here we see Capricorn with Saturn ruling. Saturn is a planet that brings boundaries and limitations, indicating conservative relationships and few truly loyal friends. In relationships, the self-sacrificing ego of the Piscean Age is apt to be self-negating, so that as friends these people often bring little of real self in communion with others.

The *Twelfth House* is the house of seclusion, the unconscious and hidden things. It is under the sign of Aquarius with Saturn and Uranus ruling. This house of the unconscious lies just back of the First House, which is the ego house. If we collectively repress into the unconscious what we do not want to look at in our society, then what is hidden there is of our own making.

For nearly two thousand years we have not dealt with the opposites. All emphasis has been on the light, the masculine, thinking and spirit side. Darkness, the feminine, feeling and substance have been pushed out, dishonored. People today are expressing their feelings which come as love and caring, but also anger, hate, and evil. What has so long been ignored, though it resides in each of us, is now emerging without restraint—from individuals as well as groups. In this long needed expression of feeling, however, the conscience does not seem to be operating as an inner check.

Jung said to a colleague not long before his death, "I don't envy anyone having to live through the end of the twentieth century." For ignoring the negativity and evil that are in the unconscious of each of us we are paying dearly. We are paying with guns, drugs, terrorists, and diseases, with poverty, illiteracy, and fascism.

People alive today have their own ideas, experiences, and responses around the Piscean Age, for this era is not yet ended. And though it is hard to be objective about what is so close, in your mind you might wish to add to what has been said here.

THE SECOND MONTH OF A GREAT NEW YEAR:

THE AQUARIAN AGE

Chapter Four

We now move to the second month of this Great New Year, the Aquarian Age. What are the new steps, now beginning to be evident, that must be taken in these next two thousand years? The symbol of the age is the mature person, indicating an evolutionary thrust toward new consciousness about ourselves and our relationships with others. Jung said that while we know much about so many things, we have little understanding of humanity and know next to nothing about ourselves. This new age makes increased consciousness an imperative for human beings.

In this last century, many people have served the planet by helping humans increase their knowledge of themselves and the world. In science, we remember Pasteur, the Curies, Einstein, Niels Bohr, Pauli; in literature, we think of Joyce, Auden, T.S. Eliot, Virginia Woolf; in religion there are Pope John XXIII, Niemöller, Martin Buber, Teilhard de Chardin; in social action, we are grateful to Gandhi, Eleanor Roosevelt, Martin

Luther King, Jr. To this list, we need to add the Wright brothers, who put transportation into the air, and two outstanding psychologists, Sigmund Freud, who made the unconscious and dreams a legitimate field of study, and Carl Jung, who pressed forward with the notion of individuation, or the idea of the mature, integrated person. Many others known and unknown in these and other fields helped increase the consciousness of this last century to make ready for the next age.

It has been said that psychology and astrology are the sciences of the new Aquarian Age. Why is this so? Because they both can tell us the most about ourselves and humankind. Used in combination, depth psychology and our astrological charts can help us know and experience things about ourselves that have been unknown. Although we do not know what this greater knowledge of self and others can mean in the development of future collective values, we are pushed by energies greater than ever before toward the pursuit of consciousness.

Spiritual forces are growing, expanding horizons in many directions. For example, we know that three dominant religions—Judaism, Christianity, and Islam—share similar histories, values, sacred texts, and holy places. The followers of these religions all believe in the same God. Given this common origin, we know that it is possible to eliminate the barriers and boundaries that now separate these faiths from one another.

Science and religion are beginning to move through their conflicts, too, for science now shows us that the only difference between what the world calls "matter" and "spirit" is one of frequency. Matter is spirit at a low frequency or spirit made manifest. Matter, then, is truly spirit-matter. In essence, all is a manifestation of a primary Source which continuously expresses itself through an infinite variety of forces.

In light of this knowledge which science has given us, we see that the planet, the material world, desperately needs human consciousness. The earth needs humans to understand the spirit that is within her, so that she might, in turn, nourish the spirit that is within each human, now possible as never before.

As the influence of Aquarius begins to be felt, many people are choosing psychotherapy to find meaning or fulfillment of life, instead of only turning to it in a crisis situation. In the process of psychotherapy, one can meet the unconscious where positive potential as well as much personal pain wait for recognition and transformation. The range of personal awareness expands, until the world is seen in a different light, and one begins to help bring the changes for which Aquarius stands.

In 1948, when a friend of mine gave a talk in London on B.B.C., an astute young woman in attendance asked her if she had done any work in depth analysis. My friend replied that she had

had several years of Jungian analysis. The young woman explained that depth analysis is usually reflected in the way a person speaks: prepared talks are not full of opinionated statements; there are no racist, sexist or ethnocentric remarks; there is little evidence that projections control the person's thought processes.

People who work on the inner world seem to develop a balanced relationship to their unconscious, so that they see a more authentic reality in others. What a step forward if every person who works with people could deeply relate to the unconscious—both personal and collective! Imagine what the world would be like if every teacher, social worker, politician, policeperson, lawyer, doctor, clergy, and others in the helping professions could achieve this knowledge of the self, this dialogue with the deepest parts of the inner world! Such self-understanding is possible.

Now to look at other qualities in this new Age of Aquarius. The sign of Aquarius is a fixed air sign with Uranus and Saturn as rulers. Belonging to the fixed quadruplicity, Aquarius joins Taurus, Scorpio, and Leo in completing the four fixed signs. They are fixed in that they are resistant to change, resolutely keeping to a preferred way of self-expression and out-goingness. It is hard for fixed signs to move away from preconceived ideas. This fixedness may manifest itself most often in a faithfulness to commitments and friends.

Air relates to communicativeness, which, in this age, involves the carrying and disseminating of information and ideas through groups of people. Fixed air makes one mentally creative and leads to the widespread sharing of objectives.

Uranus, one of the two rulers of Aquarius, is known as a planet of the unconscious. With Neptune and Pluto, Uranus is one of the three most remote planets now known. These three planets are also the most recently discovered. The other seven planets have been known since ancient times. Saturn, the other ruler of Aquarius, was the furthermost planet from the sun known to the ancients.

In their roles as rulers, Saturn and Uranus are quite dissimilar. Saturn is a traditional planet that indicates caution, limitation, sense of timing, and responsibility. It would be expected that, in this next age, these qualities will hold, reducing the chance of change in areas of life that have been workable for all people. Uranus, with its unconventionality and independence, seems at odds with the traditional Saturn. But in fact, these two can complement each other, Saturn acting to temper the revolutionary side of Uranus; extreme ideas and actions can be modified by Saturn's determination to protect the well-being of all people. The deep longing of Uranus is that all people in the world have a sense of their own dignity and worth and live in a society that permits neither poverty nor unemployment.

The symbol of Aquarius is the adult person carrying the overflowing water jar. The unique thing about this symbol is that it is the only sign of the Zodiac represented by a mature person. The only other people represented in the Zodiacal symbols are the Gemini twins who, though precocious, are immature, as is the virgin in the sign of Virgo. The centaur of Sagittarius is half person and half horse. Except for the scales of Libra, all other signs are animals.

The Water Bearer, symbol of the Aquarian Age, indicates that adult persons will carry their own living water, which is the same as saying they will hold their own redemption. The flow of water is beyond reason, suggesting the intuitive, inspirational aspects of consciousness. The water is poured from the pitcher without discrimination, as indication that Aquarian people will be interested and concerned about humanity as a whole. They will respect all persons, and the flow of their achievements will help the less fortunate ones. The spontaneity of ideas which comes with Uranus also makes for a profound inclusiveness of thought.

This is the first time in twenty-five thousand years that there has been an Aquarian Age, making it the first time Uranus, as a ruler of Aquarius, has had an effect on a Great Age. As never before, if we respond to the energies of the time by working to bring about this change of attitude, there will be a concern for the equality of people. Even though this idea is the foundation for our Bill of Rights, we have not lived the value of human rights. It is disturbing to see how racism prevails at the end of this Piscean Age.

The glyph for Aquarius is ♒, waves, yes, but air waves, not water waves. These are air waves that function through the telephone, wireless, radio and television. In this new age, great energy will be available for developing even more sophisticated forms of communications and related technologies.

The sign that complements Aquarius as its opposite is Leo, the Lion, whose regal bearing and heart-centeredness makes him known as the royal beast. Ruled by the Sun, Leo is a fixed fire sign and brings desire and enthusiasm for life. The Leonine person is dominating in leadership and organization, fixed in ideas, whole-hearted in feeling and creativity.

The qualities of leadership and organization that are natural to Leo will be important assets to Aquarius in this age when social concern for humanity will require certain changes in consciousness. While money and possessions have held power over people in this time, leaving millions without food, shelter or work, Uranus and his humanitarian energies will work for equality and respect for all people in the next age.

Fire signs, through their capacity for vitality, passion, and will, can inspire the deepest expressions of religion. Leo projects more strength and stability than Aries and Sagittarius, the other two fire signs, principally because it is ruled by the Sun. As the Sun is acknowledged as the prime source of all manifestations of earthly energies, we can expect changes in the spiritual nature of the Aquarian Age. At the very least, there will be an evolution of human consciousness.

The rapid pace of developing technology also requires greater consciousness so that we can anticipate the destructive as well as the creative aspects of each new achievement. Technological advancements have given us many gifts, but the result is that we must live with air pollution, a growing hole in the ozone layer, contaminated land and water, diminishing resources, and much more. We need to realize the opposites in every step taken, the productive and disastrous sides to each advance made. These opposites must be held in consciousness so that all steps toward newness can be taken appropriately.

This New Age requires that humankind conquer air with air, that is, with energies taken from substance in the airy state. The Wright brothers realized this possibility, using gas, mixed with air, to power their flying machine. Though people had envisioned flying for hundreds of years, the reality of flight had to wait for the proper time, that is, just a few years before this next Great Age.

Airspace has no boundaries, making it quite

possible that national boundaries will disappear in the next age. The problem with having no boundaries can be seen in the thousands of planes flying millions of miles all over the world, in the number of near air collisions because control of airways is lacking, and in the threat of war caused by ambiguities surrounding a country's airspace. On the other hand, the fact of no boundaries may force us to create a centering point for the planet. More and more we are hearing people speak of "one world," one earth, and a global consciousness. It could be that the boundaryless phenomenon of the air age, as well as Uranus' humanitarian energies, will bring about one world sooner than we expected.

Let us take a specific look at the Twelve Houses of this Aquarian Age in relation to the facets of life that they touch. Some of the houses will affect life more fully than others.

Where the glyph for Aquarius falls is the *First House*, which refers to the collective ambiance of the people for the next two thousand years. Because the symbol is the adult person, there will be a great urge among people to become whole. Persons will be more concerned about being uniquely themselves, complete individuals. To be "an individual in community" is to participate in the Aquarian ideal, for it is necessary to know one's inner wounds, complexes, and potentials to be a productive part of a community. When communities fail, it is because this knowledge of self is lacking.

The mystic, Nicholas of Cusa, has God say, "Know thyself and I shall be thine." Persons related to the unconscious as well as the conscious mind know their own needs and have an inner authority and integrity. They embody an awareness that values thoughts and feelings as much as deeds. Finally, they are objective people with a deep sense of the reality beneath those layers of illusion created by collective thought.

The *Second House* has Pisces, a water sign, with Jupiter and Neptune ruling. Jupiter will encourage more spiritual values and provide inspiration to love one's self and others. This means that compulsive acquisition, so characteristic of the Piscean Age, will give way to a flowing compassion for life itself. Instead of being egocentrically concerned about image, the Aquarian may become aware of needs that come from the inner self. By loving oneself in this deep and authentic way, one can love others.

The *Third House* is the house of communication and intellectual attitudes. The sign is Aries, which is ruled by Mars. The technological mind-set of this last century could continue to develop, given the Martian energy in this house. As Archibald MacLeish said, "The problem with this technological age is if it is possible to do something we go ahead and do it. We never ask is it what we need or is it the right thing to do. We do not question the moral quality of our actions.'' In other words, if we can make a car that goes 180 miles an hour, we make it, not asking about purpose or result; if we can tamper with human genes, we proceed, regardless of the consequences. We do not ask if our actions will lead to a better world.

Aries, a pioneering sign, pushes to be on the razor's edge in mechanical things as well as spiritual matters. The aggressiveness and thrust of Mars could continue to prevail with the attitude of ''if we can do it, it is right.'' However, the basic quality of Aquarius to respect all people and the new availability of spiritual energies might together bring a new moral consciousness to technological developments.

The *Fourth House* for the age of the Water Bearer is very different from the Pisces' Gemini sign. In this next age it will be Taurus ruled by Venus that tells us about our home and rootedness. Taurus, a fixed earth sign, can give considerable solidity and substance to this house along with a new awareness of the Earth, our real home, as a living organism. With Venus as the ruler here, we may appreciate the Earth more deeply and relate to her more than ever as the goddess she really is.

Venus indicates that feelings rather than thinking will be honored. All kinds of art and imaginative use of color will enliven the home, expressing warmth and beauty as well as a new simplicity. Because Taurians love green and growing things, homes will most likely continue to be filled with lush plants.

The *Fifth House* has the sign of Gemini ruled by Mercury and expresses the creativity of a person. Embodied by artists, authors, musicians, parents, and teachers, creativity will thrive in this house. It will also stimulate lovemaking as well as other pleasures, such as games and sports. Gemini curiosity can be extremely creative in trying new things. It could extend itself to racing, gambling, and other games of chance, which would not seem the creative way to go.

There is a particular change in the *Sixth House* if we compare the Aquarian Age to the Piscean Age. This is the house of daily work and health and has the sign of Cancer, a cardinal, feminine, water sign, being ruled by the Moon. You may remember that Leo, with the Sun ruling, was the sign over this house in the Piscean Age. Cancer, as a cardinal sign, is also an initiatory sign, and like water it is feminine. The Moon, its ruler, is the most feminine planet in the Zodiac. Altogether, this promises that we will be more related to our bodies as substance. In the past, there has been little to encourage us to honor our bodies as sacred vessels that carry our uniqueness and make possible what we do.

Like the Moon, we will be more changeful, liking our work but also enjoying and planning for more leisure. This may not always be felt, especially in the corporate world where employees work hard far more than the forty hours a week. But already there is a trend among young people to leave demanding firms, despite impressive salaries, in order to have more time off. People are asking for and receiving half-time positions as never before. Even though one must work to live, other values want to be served over constant work and the accumulation of wealth. Young people are realizing that more leisure is important for health, for cultural values, education, and introversion. In the field of work, the lunar waxing and waning is favored over the constancy of the Sun, thus complementing the evolutionary process of the Aquarian person.

The feminine principle has an all-inclusive attitude toward health and is already reflected in today's holistic medical practices. Natural childbirth is accepted and desired by many women who want to avoid the sterility of hospitals. Though medical specialists are still necessary in many cases, the feminine principle looks for ways disease can be prevented, relating to the body through instincts and intuitions. Exercise, sensible living and natural foods, used instinctively in ancient times, are recognized as the formula for health and long life—evidence of the nurturing, feminine quality of the Moon as it guides the Aquarian person. With these changes in attitude toward the body, we see that people may live to be a healthy ninety or a hundred years old during the Aquarian Age.

It takes the feminine principle in both men and women to recognize when the relationship to one's inner world is out of balance—to feel fears, anxieties, guilts, and other disturbing affects which signal the need for centering. Again, this means that more people will turn to psychotherapy and astrology to help the health of their inner worlds. It is important to remember that the words health, healing, whole, and holy are all from the same root word. To be whole is to be more holy.

We now move into the *Seventh House*, which has to do with partners and marriage. The sign of Leo with the Sun as its ruler is in this house, indicating that real relationship is of major concern in the new age rather than daily work which was emphasized in the Piscean Age.

Through depth psychology we know how much projection is a basis for falling in love. The man unconsciously projects his image of the ideal woman onto his fiancee and the woman unconsciously projects her image of the ideal man onto her partner. This situation may last one year or longer. But sooner or later, the humanness and reality of each one of the couple emerges with all the shadow elements, leaving the marriage anything but smooth. If the two people in this situation are mature enough and find real love for each other, beyond the projected qualities, they will realize that there is no real relationship without adjustment, confrontation, and much work. If there is not real value and love found in the marriage, they will divorce or live in an uncreative marriage. Real relationship has to be worked on to be achieved.

The way one functions in the *Seventh House* has been the most unconscious because it is farthest from the First House, which is the ego house. The ego is the organ of consciousness. Now illuminated by the Sun, the full light of consciousness is entering this house of relationship and marriage, making it possible for people to know enough about themselves and each other to meet as two individuals on their way to maturity. It will take some time for the collective to achieve this kind of wholeness. Nevertheless, it is rewarding to see the increasing number of couples meeting in integrity, establishing a self-to-self relationship. After the sexual promiscuity and experimentation of the sixties and seventies, many are now expressing the desire for real relationship and are willing to work for it. The idea of marriage and then "living happily ever after" is not part of the thinking of this new generation. They know that marriage is work, suffering, and sacrifice. Piscean romantic illusions are dissolving under the light of Aquarian consciousness.

The *Eighth House* is the house of sacrifice, death, and rebirth. Here we find the sign of Virgo ruled by Mercury. Immediately we see that the virgin is no longer perceived to be the ideal mate as during the Age of the Fishes. A consequence of this change from reverence for the virginal to more open sexual mores is that fewer people are joining religious orders with their commitment to vows of chastity.

How can something so subtle as this be indicated by an astrological configuration? This is the mystery we do not begin to understand.

The rationality of Mercury, or that which refuses to accept what cannot be explained, is sacrificed in this Eighth House. This opens the new age person to the irrational side which is so favored by Aquarius and so frowned upon by literal Pisces. Because of this sacrifice of Mercury's rationality, we may grow more responsive to the "synchronistic event." This is defined by Jung as an acausal happening whereby an inner need occurs simultaneously with an outer manifestation of that need. Now that we are aware of the possibility of synchronistic events, we may notice them more often, especially as our consciousness grows.

As described previously, the Eighth House is a bridge to the *Ninth House*, or the house of religion, here occupied by Libra with Venus ruling. The sacrifice of Piscean rational Mercury allows for the loving and compassionate expression of a mature Venus who, being a very feminine planet and influencing both men and women, brings us knowledge about relationship, love, beauty, and the arts. Now the religion of love will manifest itself as a mature reality rather than as the illusion it has been been during the Piscean Age. When the irrational is allowed its share of energy, we will be able to accept these loving, relational qualities of Libra with Venus ruling. Greater inner depths can be known and expressed, and emphasis will be given to the spiritual quality of love toward God and Self. At last, we can live the two commandments found in Luke: Love God with all your heart, soul, strength, and mind, and your neighbor as yourself. Although many have tried to love God and neighbor during the Piscean Age, the state of the world today suggests that the majority have not achieved such charity. And have we really loved ourselves? It may take time and work to love ourselves first, so that we will have a basis for loving others. Self-knowledge is the way to cultivate love for the Self and so offers us a place to begin our journey toward wholeness.

Scorpio with its rulers of Mars and Pluto will be found in the *Tenth House*, which has to do with the outer world and profession. Scorpio is a sign that tears down easily but also regenerates. It has a great antipathy toward anything phony or too deeply established. Those institutions that are not functioning on the basis of integrity or with concern for what is best for the people on the planet may well be pulled down unless they find in the regenerative quality of Scorpio a more humanitarian way to function.

Already there are some corporations which accept all employees as shareholders, as recognized voices in the organization of labor. Such regard for the equality and dignity of all people can only result in workers feeling more positively toward their work as well as the elimination of widespread hunger, poverty, unemployment, racism, terrorism, and even war.

As we have seen elsewhere, Mars is an aggressive planet and can move in where he feels a chance to use his energy. Pluto likes change in individuals as well as society. And he is not very predictable. If change does not come readily, he is perfectly capable of forcing it in a violent way. Very likely Mars and Pluto energy will move to tear down dictatorships that exist at this time.

Scorpio, though a water sign, has a great intensity about it. As has been said, it is the only sign of the Zodiac that has two symbols. One is the Scorpion which bites its own tail, representing the degeneration that one can fall into through dislike and rejection of oneself as a person. The other extreme is found in the symbol of the eagle. It is a classic soul bird, symbol of apotheosis, and is associated with the sun-god, fire and lightning. Maybe in the time ahead the third point between these two extremes can be achieved by the majority of the people, resulting in both mature individuals and creative relations between them.

The *Eleventh House* with its emphasis on friendship has in it Sagittarius, a mutable fire sign, with Jupiter ruling. Friendships will be centered around mutual interests and values, probably of a spiritual nature, given the influence of Jupiter. Already we see people working together to bring about the values for which they stand, although it could be happening on a much greater scale. Housing projects, peace networking, shared work around the preservation of wilderness areas and wildlife all serve as examples of this new kind of spirit-infused, value-oriented friendship.

One thinks often of the *Twelfth House* as the house of the unconscious, as it lies behind the First House which is the ego house that portrays the personality. It can also indicate what is in the unconscious for an individual to work on and relate to. In the case of the collective, however, what is in the unconscious is most likely to remain there, unacknowledged.

The Twelfth House is thought of as the house of solitude, prison, and hidden things. That which we keep hidden often keeps us in prison and must be dealt with in solitude. This house may contain what could be called the karma of a family. Karma includes those difficult parts of personality that are passed on from generation to generation. Sometimes one member of a family is conscious enough to deal with the problem and to exorcise it by working on the unconscious in depth analysis. Such family problems are also reflected in one's astrological chart, providing the knowledge for change and transformation. In T.S. Eliot's play, *The Family Reunion*, we see Harry, the son, attempting to end his family's unconsciousness. When such a family member works on a problem that has been manifesting itself for one, two, or three generations, it is possible not only to end the transmission of the problem to unborn children but also to heal the parents of the family member who is working on consciousness in the area of the karmic problem.

During the Piscean Age the sign of Aquarius was in this House of imprisoned qualities. This irrational, unconventional sign could not function as a collective attitude, leaving Piscean people very rational and concerned about collective, conventional attitudes. "What will people think?" is a phrase that many of us grew up with.

In the Aquarian Age, Capricorn ruled by Saturn is in the Twelfth House. Saturn is a planet related to time and boundaries. With Saturn in prison, people of the Aquarian Age will live more in the now, by eternal time, rather than in Saturn time, the kind of clock time which harrasses and drives people to compulsive behaviors. As for boundaries, they do not exist in the air. And again the imprisonment of Saturn is felt, so that the pull of gravity has lessened, allowing humankind to move into outer space as well as inner space. Undoubtedly, both realms will be explored to a greater degree than ever before in this new age. It is interesting to note that very near the time the Soviets sent up the first Sputnik, in the late 1950's, Jung published the first autobiography of the inner world, *Memories, Dreams, Reflections*. Both outer and inner space were penetrated further than either had been before—pointing out the mandate to be aware of and to work with the opposites.

In dealing with the unconscious, with the opposites within us, we must use our consciousness—our ego-self. As we work with the opposites in the unconscious, we find the third point between them; we integrate them and move toward wholeness. We build a bridge to the Self, which is the place of the immanent God, the *imago Dei*, the image of God that is within us. This is the work of individuation.

El Greco, the artist, is an example of one who worked to find his unique Self. He was born on Crete, which brought him close to the Byzantine stylized art of the Greek Orthodox church. Realizing that the art of his native land was not his own, he went to Venice and then to Rome, studying the artists he found in each place. His searching, religious nature drove him on to Spain, where no set art style had developed. There he found the necessary solitude, and as El Greco, the Greek, he found through his love of God what the Self in him was needing. There emerged for him a style that expressed in its verticality the spiritual longings of his soul. One could say he found himself.

A life not dominated by collective values, but guided by the inner needs of one's psyche, can touch values of a supranatural nature that lead to an evolving consciousness. To do this one needs solitude. One needs to find meaning in suffering and hardships that may come, for it is only through these difficulties that growth is realized. Such work creates an inner structure within which we can experience a sense of freedom and follow our inner authority. It is the ability to meet changes that is the concern of the evolving person. Such a one will become the redeemed mature person of the new age whose living water flowing from the jar will help those who are less fortunate on this Earth.

JESUS AS THE
AQUARIAN PERSON

Chapter Five

From the patterning of the Aquarian Age that has already begun to emerge, we can see that a new intellectual approach to life—one very different from that of the Piscean Age—will be valued. It is an approach which is based on a meeting between the conscious ego and the great potential of the unconscious rather than assumptions, illusions, partial truths, and one-sidedness, all of which come from an egocentric ego. This kind of ego does not make claims on "reality" or "truth." In any situation, where the real ego has chosen the way, there is always an opposite choice, and in between this ego-choice and its opposite are many other choices. In the Aquarian Age, with whole persons functioning from their greater potential rather than from their limited egos, the full range of possibilities may be examined before a final choice is made. One-sidedness will give way to multiple points of view.

This age of the Water Bearer implies that humankind will grow into a maturity that will result in a humanitarian attitude toward all of life on earth—toward the universe itself. Not by any stretch of the imagination can we say that this is the kind of world we live in today. Strife, torture, fighting, continual threat of total war, poverty, famine, unemployment all over the world—this is the situation we face today.

What has led us to this darkness? What keeps us from responding to the call of Aquarian Age consciousness? Jung once said that at the core of any neurosis of an individual is a religious problem, a spiritual need. Perhaps it is right to apply this principle to the masses of people on this planet. The symbols that have held spiritual value for us in the past no longer carry meaning. The quality of thinking needs to change.

Let us look at some of the symbols and beliefs that once satisfied spiritual needs but that no longer carry value for the new age person. Christianity taught that Jesus died for our sins, and that if we believed in Jesus Christ, the Messiah, our sins were forgiven and we were redeemed. This idea and ideal of salvation was projected onto Jesus Christ for nearly two thousand years. As a symbol, Jesus Christ had the meaning and strength to make Christianity the dominating religion of the Western world for most of the Piscean Age.

But what is the reality of the words "if you believe"? The expression has a vagueness, a mistiness that cannot be exactly grasped. One can assume one believes or even feel one believes, but where does change come for the individual through believing? What is one growing toward?

An air sign indicates emphasis on the intellect. As people have developed more discriminating minds, they have questioned traditional Christian principles. Can Jesus Christ forgive sins? Can he bring redemption? Furthermore, if he can forgive sins and redeem life, is it right that he should? Is it right that humans be so passive about their souls' growth and salvation?

People have also questioned the Christian concept of an all-loving God, especially in light of human events both past and present. What became of the God of the Hebrew scriptures? The God whose name could not be spoken, the God of Horeb-Sinai, the "I am that I am"—the God who was worshipped with awe and whose wrath was feared as a force equal to his mercy?

The advent of a new sign of the Zodiac is seen as a new step of God. With each new step, religious symbols, ritual, dogma, and thinking change. And so it is that the energies of the new age allow us to question old beliefs and to embrace new ways of knowing. Many people feel an urgency to understand what is needed in this movement from one step to another.

In the past fifty years, a large number of books have been written on Jesus of Nazareth, who lived and taught in pre-Christian times, and was never a Christian but a Jew—rooted in his own tradition. Is it possible that the message of

Jesus is for now and that now may become a post-Christian era?

When we first see Jesus of Nazareth in the Synoptic Gospels he had come to the movement of John the Baptist by the Jordan River. John was in the wilderness preaching that baptism was necessary for repentance unto the remission of sins. His message was an apocalyptic one; it said that each person must undergo a great change in order to bring forth fruit worthy of repentance. Those who did not bring forth fruit would be burned with an unquenchable fire. Destruction would come by the element of the past age—fire. Salvation would come through baptism by water, the element of the Piscean Age. This was still the Piscean Age. In John's message a split between good and evil was continued. The good were saved, the evil ones destroyed.

The event of the baptism of Jesus is recorded directly in few words. Jesus came from Nazareth to be baptized by John in the Jordan. Why did he come? We can only speculate. Was it curiosity? Was he feeling the need of redemption? Was it because John was outside the collective, and, therefore, compatible to him? There are many possible reasons.

"And straightaway coming up out of the water, he saw the heavens rent asunder, and the Spirit as a dove descending upon him, and a voice came out of the heavens, 'Thou art my beloved Son, in thee I am well pleased.'"

This numinous experience, told so briefly, not only changed the world but is still resounding through the universe. And yet it is seldom looked at by the Christian church for what it truly was. It appears to me as a mandala experience. Here is the coming of wholeness into a selected psyche; human consciousness leaps forward, as it were, growing beyond what had ever been before. Jesus appears to be a kind of mutation from the future, a person so evolved as to be a stranger in his own time and yet whose life exemplified the fullness of human possibility.

True to the patterning of a mandala, the baptism experience contains four episodes: Jesus descended into the water; he ascended to behold the heavens rent asunder; the spirit as a dove came into him; the voice came from above saying, "Thou art my beloved Son, in thee I am well pleased." The submersion into the silt-filled water of the Jordan River meant nothing less than facing the darkest possibilities of life, including death itself, both literal and symbolic. It is necessary to have a deep experience of inner death if one is to be reborn.

With devotion and willingness Jesus faced this complex act of descent and ascent. It resulted in the "rending of the heavens"; God could now come closer to those of His creation and be experienced by all who tried to know Him. The spirit came into Jesus as a dove, and in this gentle feminine way, the incarnation took place.

When spirit unites with spirit/substance, it becomes the Holy Spirit. The voice articulated the result of this union—the birth of a beloved child of God.

We encounter innumerable opposites within this experience: descent and ascent; the union of spirit/substance and spirit, which is also the union of the feminine and masculine; water and air; darkness and light; death and birth.

The result of this unique experience is the emergence of the Father, Holy Spirit, and Son for the first time. But what is here, in the birth of this Son, that is not in the Christian Jesus Christ? It is the darkness, encountered in the descent, that is omitted from the light-bright concept of the Christ. Also the feminine, represented here by both the baptismal waters and the dove, which as Aphrodite's bird, has not had its appropriate place in traditional Christianity. Many levels of the feminine have been left out.

In the annunciation story (Luke 1:26-38), the angel Gabriel comes to Mary to tell her she will give birth to a son who will be named Jesus. She says, "How shall this be, seeing I know not a man?" She is told that the Holy Spirit will come upon her and the power of the Most High will overshadow her. "Wherefore also that which is to be born shall be called holy, the Son of God."

We see in the baptism of Jesus the same mythic elements that are present in the annunciation story and most other creation stories: the feminine; the impregnation by the Holy Spirit; the birth of the Divine Child. In Jesus' baptism, God is born in him; the Self comes alive for him in this moment. From that time forward, he is in touch with the divine inside himself. Jung said that when an unknown part of the psyche is wakened and united with the Holy Spirit, the Divine Child is born—that is, a part of the Self comes into consciousness.

Immediately after the baptism, Jesus is "driven" into the wilderness by the Spirit. No longer gentle as a dove, the Spirit now is forceful and hard. Does this suggest that the Spirit is masculine as well as feminine?

In each aspect of the baptism, Jesus' relation to the opposites is clearly balanced. Unlike John the Baptist, whose preaching divided good and evil, keeping all opposites apart, Jesus' life shows him relating one side to the other, always looking for a third point. Unfortunately, Christianity followed John the Baptist's rather than Jesus' example. It repressed the dark side of consciousness, either pretending it did not exist or projecting it onto others. As a consequence, Christians have been expected to express only the bright, good side of consciousness. It seems that the Piscean psyche has been too much a part of the unconscious to have the objectivity necessary to deal with inner and outer opposites.

During this last century, on the eve of the Aquarian Age, we have acquired the knowledge and tools that will allow us to know about the un-conscious—that will show us how to integrate un-lived opposites in our psyches so that we can become more whole persons.

How was Jesus, who lived two thousand years ago, so aware of this need to live in right re-lationship to the many forces within the psyche? Although he tried to make himself clear to the people of his time, they were so identified with the unconscious that they could not separate from it. They lacked the objectivity necessary to relate to the unconscious. The way to be con-scious about the unconscious is to know that one's ego is separated from it. Knowledge about any given thing is possible only through separa-tion from the thing itself. It being a water age (and water represents the unconscious), they were invaded by it.

After the numinous experience of the bap-tism, Jesus was related to the image of God within, the *imago Dei*, as Jung would say. Jesus, called by many people a mutation, was like no other person known to live before his time. Though he often implied in his teachings, "what I do you can do also," he was not understood. What brought Jesus to a unique consciousness?

Jesus was steeped in his Jewish background. We know this from his continual reference to the Hebrew Scriptures and other teachings of Israel. The Israelites were longing for a messiah and be-lieved one would come to give them political freedom from Rome, and, more especially, a savior who would take away their sins and redeem them in the sight of God. This idea of the messiah-to-come was so deep in the thinking of his people that Jesus may have wondered, after the baptism, if the voice from heaven meant that he was to be the expected messiah? When the Holy Spirit drove him into the wilderness, it was this idea that Jesus may have had to wrestle with. "He was with the wild beasts; and the angels ministered unto Him," says the gospel according to Mark. (1:13) Jesus was struggling with his own dark side while being ministered to by a protective force.

There were three so-called temptations presented to Jesus at this time. First, he was to turn stones into bread; second, he was to throw himself from the pinnacle of the temple to prove he was the Son of God; third, he was shown all the kingdoms of the world and told he could have them all if he would worship Satan.

None of these are evil things in themselves. All were images that Jesus' people had associated with the messiah to come. The Jews expected the messiah to make sure they had enough to eat. As one who nourishes the people, the messiah was believed to be invincible; God would protect him no matter what he did. Lastly, the messiah would see that Israel became a theocracy. With their religion and state united, they would be protected from foreign rule.

How many of us live life according to images provided by the collective? We want to be the great peacemaker, the best parent, the wise teacher, the fine gardener, lawyer, or engineer. If we live to fulfill an image, we are living by collective values and are not fulfilling our inner patterning. Jesus' consciousness made him know that to live in response to the collective expectation of his time would not be as God's "Word" would want it.

Why did Jesus say, only after he had rejected the three temptations, that they were of Satan? And what does Satan represent for Jesus in this particular context? Jesus understood the expectations of his contemporaries, and Satan's questions made them even more clear for him. But he rejected these expectations because they represented the values of collective thinking. They did not reflect his own highest value, which, as a Son of God, he needed to manifest. Destined to live his own truth, Jesus could not accept the choices given by Satan because they did not come from his own individual self. They were the values of the unconscious majority.

What relation does Satan have to God? The questions Satan asked of Jesus helped to sharpen and define what was the will of God, or the highest value, in that situation. Can we say, then, that Satan is the other side of God? In the Adam and Eve myth, the serpent, as the other side of God, asks the question which clarifies

what God wants and needs, which is consciousness, though He Himself is ambivalent about it at
this early time. Satan only becomes evil when his
choice is followed. If Satan is the other side of
God, then God is darkness as well as light. Such
an inclusive God, who embodies the opposites
and was the God of Jesus, is very different from
the traditional Christian God whose being has
had no place for darkness.

Jesus left the wilderness knowing that he
could not be the outer messiah, expected and
wished for by his people. But in no way did he
discard the image. Knowing how necessary it is
to embody forgiveness and live a redemptive life,
he carried these values of the messiah inwardly,
relating to them in everything that he did and
said. He knew that others could live similarly, in-
forming their thoughts, words and deeds with
the image of the messiah, taking the values of the
child of God inwardly and making them their
own. He knew that mature people carry their own
living water of redemption.

After this central experience of his life, the
baptism and wilderness time, Jesus went to Galilee preaching the gospel and teaching in the syn-
agogue at Capernaum. People were astonished at
his authority. Aware of himself inwardly and
knowing the source of his authority, Jesus embodied the maturity of one born in the Aquarian
Age.

Along the shores of Galilee, he encountered

the first four fishermen who were to become his disciples. He said, "Come ye after me and I will make you to become fishers of men." (Mark 1:17) Jesus here was using the Piscean symbols of his time as well as responding to the people most available to him, the fishermen gathered around the lake of Galilee.

The Greek letters for "Jesus Christ Son of God, Savior" spell *Ichytys*—the fish. The name refers to that which comes up out of the depths of the unconscious. The fish symbol is thus the bridge between the Christ and the psychic nature of the human where the archetype of the redeemer dwells.

Shortly after Jesus' meeting with the fishermen-disciples, the "miracle" catch of fish was made. Few today would call it miraculous, for there are many possible explanations. It could have just happened; or perhaps Jesus had an intuition about where to drop the nets. Or it could have been a synchronistic event, which would indicate an inner need of Jesus for a symbol to be manifested in the outer situation.

Because of this great draught of fishes where none were to be found during the whole night of toiling, the event was overwhelming for Simon Peter. He knelt at Jesus' feet saying, "Depart from me for I am a sinful man." (Luke 5:8) Peter recognized the authority and value in Jesus and feared it. Simon and the four fishermen were told that there was nothing to fear, so they followed

Jesus as the first of the disciples and were with him until the end of his life.

The next period of Jesus' life includes several incidents that show how related he was to his Jewish roots but also how unique and individual was his own understanding of his tradition. Jesus was teaching in Capernaum in a room filled to overflowing with people. (Mark 2) Outside, four men came bearing on a pallet a man sick of the palsy. When they could not get in the door, they uncovered the roof and let the sick man down in front of Jesus, who "seeing their faith," said to the man, "Son, thy sins are forgiven." The words "their faith" refer to that of the sick man as well as the four who brought him.

This statement by Jesus was radical indeed, for at this time the Jews believed that illness of any kind was punishment for a sin committed. Forgiveness could only come by giving a burnt offering in the temple. The scribes sitting near Jesus thought he was blaspheming, for only God can forgive, they said. Aware of what they were thinking, that is, perceptive in an Aquarian way, Jesus said to the scribes, "Is it easier to say to the sick man 'Thy sins are forgiven' or to say 'Arise, take up thy bed and walk'?"

"But that you may know that the Son of man hath power on earth to forgive sins,' he said to the sick of the palsy, 'I say unto you, Arise, take up your bed and go into the house.'"

"The sick man got up and took his bed and

went forth before all the people. All who saw were amazed and glorified God saying 'we have never seen anything like this.' "

The four friends as well as the sick man himself probably recognized in Jesus a healing power. But it was the healing energy in all of them—particularly in the sick man—which was awakened and enlivened. Through Jesus' being and words the sick man took on a new perspective, an awareness of the healing quality within himself which could help him rise and walk—which would take him into the fullness of life. Christianity has seen this event as a miracle rather than as the natural consequence of a change in attitude, a forgiveness of self, a new awareness of the healing power within. But it is this last perspective that belonged to Jesus and that is characteristic of the Aquarian consciousness, which knows we have to forgive ourselves before we can feel forgiven by God or by any other person from whom we are asking forgiveness. Each of us can find the Son of man, Daughter of woman, quality in ourselves if we work hard to explore the inner world through deep analysis, prayer, meditation, and creative expression. Such inner work can bring a change in attitude and result in almost instant healing at times, making it possible for each of us to transform our wounds or sicknesses and "rise and walk." This next age is going to show the inner world being explored by the average person rather than the exceptional few.

The next three events involving Jesus would not have been initiated by any orthodox Jew. Out of what inner imperative did Jesus act in these situations?

Jesus was passing by when he saw Levi at the place of toll and said to him, "Follow me," and he did. When Jesus sat down to eat with his disciples, publicans and sinners sat down with him. The scribes and Pharisees, when they saw him eating with these people, who in their eyes were outcasts, pointed out to his disciples that Jesus was eating with publicans and sinners. Jesus heard them and said to them. "They that are whole have no need of a physician, but they that are sick. I came not to call the righteous, but sinners." (Mark 2:17)

How was Jesus able to do and say what he did here? I wonder if he didn't find those at the bottom of the social ladder more open and susceptible to his message. Very likely they were more lively and interesting to be with than the uptight Pharisees. And what did he mean when he said that those who are whole do not need a physician but only those who are sick? Surely he did not think the Pharisees were whole. But of course the Pharisees believed themselves to be complete. Was this a bit of whimsy on Jesus' part? He was calling the sinners who obviously had psychological problems instead of somatic problems, a distinction many physicians do not make even today. But he was also treating all people as equal, an Aquarian gesture which was certainly foreign to the mores of his time.

The next incident occurred when John the Baptist's disciples and the Pharisees were fasting in accordance with a certain religious law. Jesus was asked why his disciples were not fasting. (Mark 2:18-22) He asked, "Can the sons of the bridechamber fast while the bridegroom is with them? As long as they have the bridegroom with them, they cannot fast. But the days will come when the bridegroom shall be taken away from them, and then they will fast in that day." Christianity has said that Jesus was talking about himself: While he was with his disciples there was no need to fast; when he would be taken away, then they could fast.

This seems to be a logical but very literal interpretation. Unless one has followed Jesus' life by examining the historical passages which record his teaching, one does not know that Jesus never put himself in the center of the situation. Nor did he ever present himself as the only one who was or could do the thing being discussed. While this incident could be an exception, it could also be that Jesus was speaking in symbolic terms. For example, when there is a wedding or an occasion which calls for celebration, those related to the event have no need to fast. It would be a time of joy and close relationship even among the Pharisees.

Following this exchange over the time of fasting, Jesus gave two short parables. They use different images but convey practically the same message.

He said, "No one sews a piece of unshrunk cloth on an old garment; if he does, the patch tears away from it, the new from the old, and a worse tear is made. And no one puts new wine into old wineskins; if he does, the wine will burst the skins, and the wine is lost, and so are the skins; but new wine is for fresh skins." (RSV, Mark 2:21-22) From these parables, we can see that Jesus feels he has a new message and knows a new and open attitude is needed to follow the new message. Although these three parables can be taken literally, as the Piscean Christian mind has done, for Jesus Christ has been the object of their devotion, the Aquarian mind regards these parables as symbolic situations to be taken inwardly.

The third episode (Mark 2:23-28) tells us that Jesus was going with his disciples through the grain fields on the sabbath. The disciples began to pluck the ears and eat for they were hungry. The Pharisees asked Jesus and his disciples why they were working on the sabbath, when it was not lawful. Jesus turned to history and talked about David, an honored king. "Have you never read what David did, when he was in need and was hungry, he and those who were with him: how he entered the house of God, when Abiathar was high priest, and ate the bread of the Presence, which it is not lawful for any but the priests to eat and also gave it to those who were with him?" (RSV, Mark 2:25-26) Then in the Markan account Jesus made a surprising statement. He said, "The sabbath was made for man, not man for the sabbath; so the Son of man is lord even of the sabbath." (RSV, Mark 2:27-28)

Here again we have the words "Son of man" as seen in the story of the palsied man. "Son of man" is a phrase found in the book of Ezekiel, and also in the later books of Daniel and Enoch. While many have thought that Jesus' use of it applied only to himself, it is more likely that Jesus used it to describe a person having a life of greater consciousness. Jesus is trying to impress the lawgivers that people must function out of a real inner need, not a rigid conviction of law.

While traditional Christianity has believed that Jesus' stories and expressions always refer to himself, close examination of the texts shows Jesus describing a way of being natural to all those who have broadened their horizons—who are not caught in projections, biases, prejudices, and compulsions. People who have worked with the opposites and have achieved a quality of selfhood that can be called supranatural, are the ones he is addressing. He knows himself and assumes others can and must do the same to be healthy persons. This statement would fit with the Sixth House for Jesus' chart, it being about daily work and health.

In all three of the above incidents, Jesus made need rather than law the basis of choosing what one does. This kind of choice cannot be made in response to egocentric need, however. It is the need of the soul to which we must respond, implying that we must know ourselves well if we are to discern what is egocentric need and what is the need of the God within us. If we are conscious choicemakers, we know the inner motives that account for what we are choosing. If we act from a sense of inner authority, we move toward the highest value in each situation.

Even now something is fermenting underneath to bring more awareness to outer situations. More people are feeling an urgent desire to do inner work, to develop awareness and find meaning in the actions of everyday life. The process is gathering momentum. This is a quality that comes from the Aquarian Ninth House of religion. The Libra sign of the scales brings justice and balance to decisions. The Venus ruler brings love and compassion for oneself and others. These ways of responding do not come out of ego desires, but from authentic need and the Self where the spark of God resides.

In the Beatitudes, Jesus talked about the poor, the hungry, and the suffering ones, each time giving encouragement about what the future holds. He portrayed the humanitarian attitude that all people need to live with dignity and enjoy the possibility of fulfillment. In these words Jesus reflected the reality of the Aquarian person found in the First House of the Aquarian Age. He .emphasized the inner world when he talked of the kingdom of God and said, "The kingdom of God cometh not with observation...the kingdom of God is within you." (Luke 17:20-21) Where God rules is not in a particular city, country, or planet, but in the heart of the person that lets him/her be supreme.

In his teachings, Jesus emphasized again and again that actual change comes about through the transformation of one's inner attitudes. This understanding of Jesus can be placed in the Aquarian Ninth House of religion. It follows, then, that he came to himself in the wilderness where he felt the need to stay related to certain values inwardly rather than projecting them onto an outer reality. When he talked about Jewish law, Jesus came to his point again: "Think not that I came to destroy the law or the prophets: I came not to destroy but to fulfill. . . . For I say unto you that except your righteousness shall exceed the righteousness of the scribes and Pharisees ye shall in no wise enter into the kingdom of heaven (God)." (Matthew 5:17, 20)

Jesus goes on to say: "Ye have heard . . . thou shall not kill, and whosoever shall kill shall be in danger of the judgment; but I say unto you that everyone who is angry with his brother shall be in danger of the judgment." (Matthew 5:21-22) Jesus never condemns a person who is angry, for anger is a part of human consciousness. But he does say that we must do something about our anger in order to transform the negative energy.

Jesus' consciousness here feels as if it comes from the First House, from his Aquarian ego that knows how to judge without being judgmental. The Uranian ruler finds life in being aware of what goes on in the inner world as well as the outer situation. This correspondence between the Aquarian ego and Jesus shows him to be a spiritual revolutionary, for although he points to the outer, literal meaning of the law he also acknowledges inner feelings that can go unrecognized or erupt in sarcasm, ridicule, masochism, and pointed slurs. In his discussion of other laws, Jesus repeats this pattern of acknowledging statements made in Hebrew Scriptures while pointing out the inner attitudes that determine whether or not one is in accordance with the true spirit of the law.

Especially worthy of our contemplation today is another of Jesus' statements: "Resist not evil." (Matthew 5:39) What was Jesus trying to tell us? How have we treated evil for two thousand years? We have said it does not exist. We have closed our eyes to it, pretending it is not there. We have run away from it, thinking that we have no evil, continuing with our "good works."

From depth psychology, we can now see that Jesus was in touch with the fact that we need to deal with the opposites within us. The more we live the "good side," automatically the more we repress the evil side, even though it is always there. What we do not know about ourselves and leave unrecognized in the unconscious is projected onto certain individuals, onto the environment, onto certain countries, nationalities, or groups of people that have standards of living different from our own. Jung expresses it this way: "Today humanity, as never before, is split into two apparently irreconcilable halves. The psychological rule says that when an inner situation is not made conscious, it happens outside as fate. That is to say, when the individual remains undivided and does not become conscious of his inner contradiction, the world must perforce act out the conflict and be torn into opposite halves." We all have these unexplored parts of darkness in ourselves. The crimes that are extant now show how much of the suppressed evil is being released into the world. But recognition of the evil in oneself is possible; as such, it would be an act of the First House where ego choices are made.

For much of this last age, feelings have been repressed. As said before, the movement of this Aquarian Age is toward the expression of feelings. But when so many negative feelings have had no outlet for so long, and finally there is opportunity for release with no constraints or boundaries, they explode dangerously. Lacking are the boundaries of an inner conscience, of parental love and direction, of church influence, and of favorable adult examples. They are boundaries which are desperately needed.

Our country does not realize, as do some other nations, that retaliation is never a cure for attack. An age that is grounded in psychological and spiritual reality will know that dialogue between equals is the appropriate response to aggression or disagreement. The movement of the Aquarian Age supports this.

One other law that Jesus comments on is this:

"Ye have heard that it was said, 'Thou shalt love thy neighbor, and hate thine enemy,' but I say unto you, Love your enemies, and pray for them that persecute you; that ye may be sons of your Father . . . for He maketh his sun to rise on the evil and the good, and sendeth rain on the just and the unjust . . . Ye therefore shall be perfect as your heavenly Father is perfect." (Matthew 5:43-45, 48)

In the above law, as Jesus states it, we may have enemies, but we should act toward them in the spirit of inclusion rather than hate. Where Jesus uses the word perfect, he means it in the Greek sense, which is "all-inclusive," rather than in the Latin sense, which is to be "without fault." Thus the difference between perfect and all-inclusive is as great as the difference between evil and good. All-inclusive means that the reality of each of us is made up of our evil as well as our good side.

How many adults, taking the goal of perfection for themselves, never become themselves because of the impossibility of being without fault? These are the people who, as parents, put an impossible burden on their children, with the idea that they should be perfect—that is, without defect. Even if parents never articulate such a value, but only carry it inside them, the child's unconscious picks it up just the same. Mother Nature is never taken in by the idea of pure goodness; she values all-inclusiveness as the foundation of her creation.

Jung once said in a conversation, "Be sure that you take your dark side to God, for that is what He needs." God wants to know our wholeness, not our partialness. And He needs to know that we know it also.

From the teachings of Jesus, we get the essence of the man. The passages that follow have to do with relationship. They are as inexorable as the laws of nature. How did he understand relationship to this degree? Could he have realized that it was to be the most emphasized part of life in the new age? Knowledge of the past, present, and future must have been his, through his relation to the unconscious, for his teachings certainly reflect an understanding of what was to come as well as what had gone before.

He said, "Judge not that ye be not judged.

For with what judgment ye judge ye shall be judged; and with what measure ye mete, it shall be measured unto you." (Matthew 7:1-2) Here he is not saying that we must not judge. Life requires us to make many judgments. Rather Jesus is alerting us to understand that when we judge we open ourselves to a judgment. Not all will agree with us or like what we stand for, so we must be prepared to stand on our own authority. It is also necessary to realize that there is a difference between judging and being judgmental in a negative way, which often happens when we are projecting.

In another familiar statement Jesus said: "Why beholdest thou the mote that is in thy brother's eye, but considerest not the beam that is in thine own eye? Or how wilt thou say to thy brother, 'let me cast out the mote out of thine eye'; and lo, the beam is in thine own eye? . . . . cast out first the beam out of thine own eye; and then shalt thou see clearly to cast out the mote out of thy brother's eye." (Matthew 7:3-5)

Jesus made this clear statement, describing a psychological phenomenon which we now call projection, almost two thousand years ago. It is amazing how many people do not yet understand that projection is the unconscious alerting us to something we don't know about ourselves. We think the problem is outside ourselves when really it is inside. We cannot—nor would we want to—stop the original projection, for it occurs so that we may be informed about something inside us that needs attention. We must see it as our own problem, as Jesus so adequately said. Can we doubt his knowledge about what depth psychology is just now helping us to understand?

The so-called Golden Rule follows closely. It is probably one of the most misunderstood statements that Jesus made about relationship. "All things therefore whatsoever ye would that people should do unto you, even so do ye also unto them: for this is the law and the prophets." (Matthew 7:12)

Have we not looked at this statement in a too literal and superficial way, making our measure something that is insignificant? For example, we say we don't want a phone call before eight o'clock in the morning, so we don't call anyone before that time. We have taken the text in a Piscean self-sacrificing way. We try to guess what others want and fail miserably, deciding, in the end, that Jesus' admonition makes no sense. But what does the Self in us want? To really know what one wants takes a maturity and a knowing of oneself that goes beyond the ego's point of view. In the Golden Rule Jesus is talking about the Self. Out of this center we know that we want to be treated with the dignity that is owed each individual; we want to be treated as children of God. If each of us held this attitude, toward ourselves and others, we could make a different world! If everyone expressed this value, there would be no more war, no more second-class citizens, no more oppression. This is the real meaning of personhood.

Beginning with what Jesus said about anger through the discussion of the Golden Rule, we have been dealing with the issue of relationship, which is the concern of the Seventh House for the Aquarian Age. Jesus' teachings seem to be following the patterns reflected in this house, and, in yet another way, show him to be a man of the new age. Remember that Leo, which is ruled by the Sun, is the sign in this Seventh House. The Sun brings the awareness that we need to be more conscious about our relationships. It will be the facet of life that will get the most attention, replacing daily work, which has been the focus of awareness during the Piscean Age.

Probably the most striking in this series of Jesus' statements is this: "Enter ye in by the narrow gate; for wide is the gate and broad is the way, that leadeth to destruction, and many be they that enter in thereby. For narrow is the gate, and straitened the way, that leadeth unto life, and few be they that find it." (Matthew 6:13-14) This is a statement of two ways and two outcomes. Jesus said that we have a choice. We want to believe that every one would choose the outcome of life, but Jesus says few are they that find it. To find life one needs to go the way of finding the real person within, one's soul quality.

This is the way of individuation.

The journey of the Self, the place of the immanent God at our center, is where we find Life. The gate is narrow, for we have to rid ourselves of inner baggage—compulsions, anxieties, fears, projections, and other unconscious manifestations. This lonely and absolutely unique way is only for the individual to endeavor. The broad way, on the other hand, has plenty of room for those who follow the trends of the times. It is for the masses and reflects the collective values. It is a way that leads to destruction.

We still do not know how to enter the narrow gate. It is not told to us in what we have just read, but in a few verses beyond, we find a succinct statement that does shed some light on the process: "Not everyone that saith unto me, Lord, Lord, shall enter into the kingdom of God; but he that doeth the will of my Father." (Matthew 7:21)

Jesus makes a clear statement here, distinctly separating himself from the Source. As he has said before, one can follow his teachings as they apply to one's life, but he cannot save another person. One must do that for oneself. To do God's will is the answer to entering the kingdom of God; and it *is* entering the narrow gate which leads to Life.

To do God's will or to act on a value related to the Source is a familiar but vague statement. I have heard people in discussion groups say, "If I thought I knew what God wanted, I would do it," or "If God told me what He wanted, then I could decide if I want to do it." Does the content of the will or the decision to do the will come first? With some thought, it becomes clear that a container has to be there in which to choose and hold God's will. The container is the conscious commitment, in a moment of full awareness, to do the will of God. If one makes this commitment, every choice—whether it involves other people or only oneself—is based on the highest value to be achieved, that is, on the greatest growth possible.

"Man was made for the sake of choice," is a statement from the Kabbalah. One makes the best choice one can at the time with the knowledge one has of oneself and the situation. It might not be the choice one would make a year later or five years later. And it may be even the wrong choice. But one must choose. As one learns more deeply about oneself, choices will be made which are more in keeping with the true value presented.

At the end of the seventh chapter of Matthew, Jesus said: "Every one therefore which heareth these words of mine, and doeth them, shall be likened unto a wise man, which built his house upon the rock; and the rain descended, and the floods came, and the winds blew, and beat upon that house; and it fell not; for it was founded on the rock. And every one that heareth these words of mine, and doeth them not, shall be likened unto a foolish man, which built his house upon sand; and the rain descended, and the floods came, and the winds blew, and smote upon that house; and it fell; and great was the fall thereof." (Matthew 7:24-27) It is evident that Jesus knew the work necessary for building on rock. Nothing worthwhile comes easily.

The core of Jesus' teachings can be found in this chapter. Entering the narrow gate, doing the will of God, working to build one's soul on the rock of self knowledge and commitment to God— these powerful images enable the ego, which belongs in the First House of the Aquarian horoscope, to choose the highest value.

To understand Jesus as an Aquarian person, one needs to look at his encounters with the sinner woman, who was quite likely Mary Magdalene, although she is not called by name in this first meeting that is recorded. Jesus had been invited to eat at the home of a Pharisee. He entered and was eating when a woman of the city, a sinner she was called, also entered the Pharisee's house, bringing with her an alabaster cruse of ointment. She came to Jesus' feet and wept, washing his feet with her tears and wiping them with her hair. She kissed his feet and then anointed them with ointment.

The Pharisee, named Simon, spoke within himself saying that surely Jesus was no prophet or he would have perceived that this woman was a sinner. Jesus, aware of Simon's attitude, said to him. "I entered your house, you gave me no water for my feet, but she has wet my feet with her tears and wiped them with her hair. You gave me no kiss, but she has not ceased to kiss my feet. You did not anoint my head with oil, but she has anointed my feet with ointment. Therefore, her sins, which are many, are forgiven, for she loved much; but he who is forgiven little, loves little." (Luke 7:44-47 RSV)

Jesus then said to the woman, "Thy sins are forgiven . . . Thy faith hath saved thee; go in peace." (Luke 7:48, 50) Only a man truly related to his own feminine side could have shown the accepting attitude Jesus does toward this woman. He was in no way threatened by her. He was able to say to her, "Thy sins are forgiven" because she had forgiven and accepted herself enough to be able to risk and complete this ritual of washing and anointing Jesus' feet. To have the courage to have been a prostitute and to enter a home where women were not invited was a terrific step for her. To ritualize it makes one feel how at peace she was within herself.

When Jesus used the word faith, which he did rarely, he meant it as an action involving a higher value or consciousness. This is not the way the word faith is used by the church, which has taken it to mean "the substance of things hoped for, the evidence of things unseen," which is Paul's definition of the word.

Because this sinner woman seemed prepared for Jesus' coming to the Pharisee's house, having her ointment ready, it would appear she had some knowledge of him, or at least had observed his movements. She must have felt he carried a value which she greatly needed. Since women were not allowed as guests in a Pharisee's house, one has to recognize the courage it took for her to proceed, not only against the dictates of the culture but against her own sense of unworthiness. What she had to overcome to enter! How tuned she was to her own soul's need! Because of his own wholeness, Jesus could meet her in her coming and recognize her need.

Mary Magdalene, believed to be this same sinner woman, was known to have joined Jesus' disciples, to have followed him to his crucifixion, and to have attended his tomb with the other devoted women. Medieval stories tell of a great love between Mary Magdalene and Jesus and these stories as they were developed in the Gnostic Gospels were deleted from the canon as inauthentic. Other records of this love were destroyed and the remembering of the accounts died out. Even so, there are other mythic accounts of Mary Magdalene being in Europe and reaching Marseilles before the end of her life. Her bones are said to rest in the church of the little village of Vézelay, France. She was the subject for many Renaissance artists as well as more modern ones, such as Rodin.

A paradox is a seemingly contradictory statement that nonetheless is true. Science talks about the wave and the particle theories that are seemingly incompatible, but that are one and the same thing, found in matter and in light. It seems that the Western mind has not used paradox as a way of thinking until recently, in response to the influence of Oriental thought. But paradoxical thinking was not unknown to Jesus. One of his statements is referred to as The Paradox: "Whosoever shall lose his life shall preserve it." (Luke 17:33) A.E. Housman said these were the most profound words ever to be spoken.

To understand this statement fully, one must look at the Greek. The first half of the paradox, "Whosoever shall seek to gain his life shall lose it," means he who builds walls around his life shall lose life. How do we build walls around our life? Is it not when we feel we cannot change but when we must remain in the deep hole of our habit patterns—or, symbolically, when we keep our boat tied to the shore and won't meet the depth of the ocean or the waves that might toss it about? With walls about our life, or with our boat tied to shore, nothing changes, and so we lose what life we thought we had. If, however, we lose the life that we had been trying to save and make life a process of choosing new patterns, we are continually growing. The finding of new resources within ourselves, the manifesting of new potentials, the letting go of old ways—this is how we give birth to a new way of life. If we are going to become the mature, whole people that the Aquarian Age holds as possibility, we have to use all parts of our psyches. Jesus' great paradox is a deeply religious statement which would be placed in the Ninth House of the Aquarian horoscope.

Soon after this statement of the paradox, it was said of Jesus: "And it came to pass, when the days were well-nigh come that he should be received up, he stedfastly set his face to go to Jerusalem." (Luke 9:51) Why did Jesus choose to go to Jerusalem? Was it possible that he was feeling that he must not stay at the periphery of the country where multitudes were following him? That he must ascertain the attitudes at the center, in the Holy City? Could it be that Jesus' movement toward Jerusalem was symbolic of his coming to his own center? Quite likely there was an inner need, a feeling that the direction he should take for his own fulfillment would come clear during this journey to the city.

His decision would have belonged in the Ninth House of the Aquarian chart, the house of long journeys, religion, and individuation, all three of which were contained for Jesus in his journey to Jerusalem. It could have been included in the Eighth House also, which is the house of sacrifice, death, and rebirth. Certainly he sacrificed his own security and the support of the large, eager multitudes that he met in the country out of Jerusalem, eventually leading to his death.

Very soon after this time, a certain man said

he would follow Jesus anywhere. Jesus responded: "The foxes have holes, the birds of the
heavens have nests: but the Son of man hath not
where to lay his head." (Luke 9:58) Jesus here
was quite likely talking about himself, but he
also could have meant any person who is living
at the supranatural level of a relationship with
the Source by doing the will of God. The patterning of the wanderer becomes apparent in the new
age, for true life is not found in home, possessions, or in staying at one place, either literally or
symbolically. Life is in mobility and newness.
Expression of this new age value can be seen in
the many young people, men and women, who
travel about with packs on their backs. Rather
than derelicts, they are often college graduates
who reject the safety of staying home to find
work; they embrace the opportunity of learning
more about themselves and life by wandering.
They realize that security can too easily become
a static goal; the way of Life is process.

In one place, Jesus was asked by the Pharisees when the kingdom of God would come. He
answered, "The kingdom of God cometh not with
observation; neither shall they say, Lo, here! or,
There! for lo, the kingdom of God is within you."
(Luke 17:20-21) Jesus showed the kingdom of
God to be an inner reality, a place one can be in
one's inwardness, the dwelling into which God
can enter if we commit ourselves to doing His
will. Every time Jesus talks about inwardness or

against negative thinking, he is speaking of an Aquarian ability rather than a Piscean attribute.

Christianity has been thought of as the religion of love and has been founded on the teachings of Jesus, who has been made into Jesus Christ, the divine son of God. The seeds for this Christian interpretation may be found in the incident involving Jesus and the lawyer who asked him how to inherit eternal life. Jesus asked the lawyer what he had read in the law, and the lawyer answered, "Thou shalt love the Lord thy God with all thy heart, and with all thy soul, and with all thy strength, and with all thy mind; and thy neighbor as thyself." Jesus answered him, "Thou hast answered right: this do, and thou shalt live." (Luke 10:27-28)

The lawyer appears to be asking about "eternal life" in the sense of chronological time or in the quantity of years to be gained. While Jesus commended the lawyer for bringing together the two commandments in the Hebrew Scriptures, he emphasized that eternal life is a quality of Life, to be lived in the here and now. To love with all one's heart, soul, strength, and mind leaves very little, if anything, out of one's total being; to cultivate these four parts of ourselves—four being the number of wholeness—is to have eternal quality of life now.

To indicate that which exists in each one of us, the immanent God who makes for the quality of life that we live, we can use other words, such as Force, Energy, Process, Source, the Eternal or the "Nothing that wants to become Something", an expression used by Jakob Böhme, the medieval mystic. I recognize that the word God might not be the word chosen by all to express the Divine that is within and without us. It is a convenient word for it is understood by most people.

We need to look at the statement, "to love your neighbor as yourself." It is said in the Hebrew Scriptures with such simplicity that we are made to think that the average person does love him or herself. While self-love may have been natural for people living during the time of the writing of the Hebrew Scriptures as well as during the time of Jesus, it is not today. They are rare persons about whom it can be said that they love themselves without working at it. If a person does seem happy with himself or herself, it is often only a mask of arrogance or egocentricity that covers great dissatisfactions and insecurity underneath. When such people do express their needs, with the claim of knowing themselves, they are often called selfish and superficial. Too few people know or follow their real needs.

We have tried to love others without loving ourselves and it does not seem that we have done it well. We have been living partial lives without relationship to the resources of the unconscious. Nothing in our religion or mores has enabled us to connect to our totality or helped us to change the images we have of ourselves. In these next centuries it is very likely that our "neighbors" will be much more extended. We already see the mobility of people in the world as they leave difficult situations in the hope of finding more opportunities in other countries. Although Christianity has taught us to believe in Jesus Christ, the Messiah, as the source of our forgiveness of sins and our salvation, Jesus of Nazareth was teaching another message.

In the wilderness, we must remember, Jesus did not discard the image of the messiah or what that person was to carry, though he knew he was not the expected one. When he left the wilderness, he knew the redemptive quality that was a messianic hope must become an inner quality—for himself and for others. Jesus lived this value of forgiveness and redemption. The rest of us are often not aware of this value in ourselves until the Self has been touched; then we know that to be a mature person means carrying our own redemption—our own living water.

The story about the Prodigal Son (Luke 15:1-32), familiar to most people, parallels the inner journey that Jung described as the way to individuation. To take any journey, outer or inner, we need to ascertain our assets. Energy, mostly in the form of money, constitutes outer needs; the inner journey requires energy, too, but energy of a different sort—the kind of energy that allows one to stay with the journey, to take the suffering as well as the joys that come, to be willing to die and be reborn. As Goethe said, "Die to become."

In this famous story, which also functions as a parable of an inner journey, the younger son departed his father's household and "went into a far country." The unconscious is a far country—alien, threatening, beautiful, compelling. "He wasted his substance with riotous living." When he returned home, his older brother accused him of devouring his living with harlots. It would seem that the phrase "wine, women, and song" is equal, in connotation, to the expression "riotous living." But is it possible that many of our less obvious obsessions are also riotous living? Obsessions for food, for cleanliness, for perfection, for accomplishment and success in all that we do? Because we are unaware of such obsessions, particularly when they are collectively correct and leave us feeling falsely righteous, the flow of our lives is blocked. They drain us and leave us without the energy we need to take the real, inner journey.

After wasting his substance, or money, which is usually a symbol of energy, the prodigal son "joined himself to one of the citizens of that country, [who] sent him into his fields to feed swine. And he would fain have been filled with the husks that the swine did eat." This suggests that the inner journey involves meeting and dealing with the negativity in one's psyche—dealing with the shadow side. Nothing is more degrading than having to confront that part of the psyche which is symbolized as swine. Nevertheless, this deeply taboo part of oneself needs complete acceptance.

Jesus spoke with integrity in this parable because, to a great extent, it could have been modeled on his own experience. Undoubtedly out of the energy of his life at home, he went to encounter John the Baptist at the Jordan, a meeting which marked the beginning of Jesus' profound inner and outer journey.

It was "when he came to himself," that the prodigal son said, "How many hired servants of my father's have bread enough to spare, and I perish here with hunger! I will arise and go to my father, and will say unto him, Father, I have sinned against heaven, and in thy sight; I am no more worthy to be called thy son: make me as one of thy hired servants." (Luke 15:17-19) To face the inner darkness and to claim it as one's own is a humbling experience. But it also opens the way to the Self, expressed here in the phrase "when he came to himself." This younger son starts his journey back to his home, but with the attitude of being a servant rather than a son. "While he was yet afar off, his father saw him, and was moved with compassion and ran, and fell on his neck and kissed him . . . for this my son was dead, and is alive again." (Luke 15:20-21, 24) One who knows nothing of the far country, the unconscious, is not truly alive. The inner depths that bring the unexpected into life go unrecognized, leaving one with only a partial existence. Here the prodigal son, having taken the way of the narrow gate and found Life, was welcomed with a celebration beyond his expectation. He was in right relationship with the father and the Father.

As we know, the older son had stayed home. He made sure he took no risks, and tried to please his father by doing what he thought was wanted. Except to become jealous and bitter, he underwent no change, having chosen the broad way that leads to destruction.

At one point in Jesus' life, he is said to have made a very obscure remark. In speaking to two of his disciples, he said: "Go into the city; and there shall meet you a man bearing a pitcher of water; follow him." (Mark 14:13) New Testament scholars and their students seem unable to discern the meaning of these words, saying only that the image of a man with a water jar must be a symbol of something. It could hardly relate to Jesus' time, for no man carried a pitcher of water in those days, such being the work of women only.

Jesus made this statement on the first day of Passover, after his arrival in Jerusalem. He knew how much danger he was in. He was aware that he was very likely facing death. Why the statement about the man with the water pitcher and the imperative to follow such a man? Did Jesus know this as the symbol of the Aquarian Age? Did he know that it represented a different consciousness than he found around him? This consciousness is expressed in everything he taught. He hoped it could be lived by the generations of his time, but he also knew that to achieve this kind of consciousness much work was necessary. It is not something we are born with; it is not natural to our development. Consciousness is achieved only as we work to manifest the Self, which is supranatural and beyond the qualities with which we are born. Jesus hoped that his teachings could be lived and expressed by others of his time. We can only try to imagine his burden and despair.

Shortly after Jesus came to Jerusalem, it was the day of unleavened bread, known as Passover. It is a day celebrated by all Jews with solemnity and joy. It was on that day that Jesus made the statement about following the man with the pitcher of water, taken today as the symbol of the Aquarian Age. This statement, found in Mark and Luke, does not appear in Matthew. (Luke is known to draw on a separate document that begins at Jesus' entrance into Jerusalem and is interspersed where Luke does not follow Mark.) In the Lukan account, in this same chapter where Jesus spoke about the man with the water pitcher, there is a most unusual statement by Jesus to his disciples:

"...I have desired to eat this passover with you before I suffer: for I say unto you, I will not eat it, until it be fulfilled in the kingdom of God. And he received a cup, and when he had given thanks, he said, 'Take this, and divide it among yourselves; for I say unto you I will not drink from henceforth of the fruit of the vine, until the kingdom of God shall come.' " (Luke 22:15-18)

Because he was a Jew, Jesus' refusal to celebrate the Passover was an amazing decision. Why did he make this statement? One must first consider the deepest meaning of the Passover—that it celebrates the passing over by the Angel of Death, during the time of Moses, those Israelite households which put lamb's blood on their doorposts and lintels. Except for these faithful Jews, all others in the land of Egypt suffered God's wrath as he sent his death angel to smite the first born of every man and beast. To the Israelites, God said, "this day you shall keep as a feast to the Lord; throughout your generations, you shall observe it as an ordinance forever." (Exodus 12:14)

This whole story indicates the Lord's patience, and his ambivalence, Moses' devotion to his people, and the Pharoah's determination not to lose his slaves. The number of plagues visited on the Egyptians were many, and still the Pharoah hardened his heart. Even after the killing of the firstborn of man and beast, he hardened his heart and pursued the people of Israel into the parted Red Sea, only to have all the pursuers drown, men and horses together.

This incident also shows how God is in the

process of gaining consciousness, just as individuals are. The statement in Exodus shows that the destroyer killed thousands of men on foot, besides women and children. Who was this destroyer, if not God?

As a Jew, Jesus knew the background of his people, including the ordinance to celebrate the Passover forever. What was his relationship to that event to make him refuse to eat and drink? One can only surmise, but he knew the political and religious climate of those days in Jerusalem. He had already said that one who sat around the table, one of the twelve, would betray him. (Mark 14:15) Jesus knew deep inside of him that his life would be taken from him. As the firstborn son of God he was not going to be passed over. It would violate his inner truth to celebrate the Passover and its deepest meaning.

At that moment of time, Jesus stood as a distinct, unique individual, unrelated to his Jewish roots and absolutely unrelated to the idea of being an object of devotion, which Christianity made of him for two thousand years. As a whole person, he could not have accepted outwardly the messianic image of forgiveness and redemption which he nevertheless carried within. The devotion of this man to his own myth, as a unique individual, is magnificent to behold here.

It is amazing that the words of Jesus, "I will not eat ... I will not drink ..." (Luke 22:16-18) have been left in the record. They undoubtedly are the words of Jesus, for no one else would have said them.

Thus, Jesus carried the value of salvation, a collective projection, through a period of two thousand years. A few rare people, probably, were objective enough at that time to carry the value in themselves. But generally speaking that maturity is left for people of the new era to achieve and develop. Jesus, as the Christ, passed through the era of being a divine symbol, as was apparently necessary during the Piscean Age. When we look at him today, and regard him as the pre-Christian person that he was, we see that he was a unique human being who taught others again and again: "What I do you can do also."

How one follows the way of Jesus is always an individual matter; he did not mean for us to live our lives exactly as he lived his. Instead, he called us each to follow our own way, as our inner integrity dictates. The projections onto Jesus that were carried by the symbol of the Jesus Christ are deep in the bones of most people in the Western world; they rest in the unconscious of those who have been raised as Christians, those who have rejected Christianity, and those who have had little or no exposure to Christianity. Jesus' words tell us about the way—not his—to achieve the Self. To do this, we must withdraw our projections from Jesus Christ the symbol and carry the values of Jesus the teacher within ourselves.

The above Lukan account of the Passover supper is amplified by Paul in Corinthians I when he had Jesus say, in effect: This is my body, this is my blood. Take in remembrance of me. (cf. I Corinthians 11:23-25) In Mark and Matthew the same words of "my body" and "my blood" are found. Mark is quoted as saying, "This is my blood of the covenant, which is shed for many. Verily I say unto you, I will no more drink of the fruit of the vine, until that day when I drink it new in the kingdom of God." (Mark 14:24-25) Matthew is quoted as using the same words as Mark, except after the phrase "for this is my blood of the covenant, which is shed for many," he or his editor adds "unto the remission of sins" and finishes with "I will not drink henceforth fruit of the vine, until that day when I drink it new with you in my Father's kingdom." (Matthew 26:29) These words have accompanied the sacrament of communion, which has had—and will continue to have—untold meaning for countless people. It is undoubtedly true, however, that they were not said by Jesus, but were developed in the ritual of the early Christian community, recorded by Paul, and then put into the gospel account of the Passover.

After the Passover supper with his disciples, Jesus left with them to go to Gethsemane. He asked most of them to sit as he prayed, but took Peter, James, and John into Gethsemane with him. To them all, he said: "My soul is exceeding sorrowful even unto death: abide ye here, and watch." He walked forward and fell on the ground to pray, addressing God in the most familiar, intimate way: "Abba, Father, all things are possible unto thee; remove this cup from me; howbeit not what I will, but what thou wilt." (Mark 14:34-36)

This material about Jesus fits into more than one house in the Aquarian horoscope. His use of "Abba" for God shows what a close relationship he had with God, for Abba in our language is equal to the familiar "Daddy." This closeness would fall in the Seventh House, the house of relationship. Jesus was quite sure his death was imminent, a consciousness which corresponds to what is required by the Eighth House, the house of sacrifice. Of course he made the greatest sacrifice he could—his own life. Even so, it was not a martyr's death, for he went voluntarily out of the depth and strength of his own religious commitment.

Jesus' prayer would be part of the Ninth House, the house of religion. He prayed what a Western prayer needs to be; he opened himself to God's will even while expressing his own. There is a place for the will of the ego to be stated in any prayer, for it indicates a knowing about oneself. But, like Jesus, our prayers should conclude with a submission to a higher will. What makes Jesus' prayer a deeply religious moment are his words, "not what I will, but what thou wilt." (Mark 14:36)

Was it truly God's will that Jesus should die?

Jesus knew that he wanted to live. Why should he want to die, a young man with a message, which, if followed, could have changed the history of the world? The strength of Jesus was great; his ego clearly knew what he wanted to do, but nevertheless he was ready to accept God's will for him. He accepted completely the cup of his own destiny—the cup that would not be removed. Jesus returned three times to the place of the disciples, and each time they were sleeping. "Couldst thou not watch one hour?" What a reality to face at this time! Following this prayer, Jesus comprehended spirit-matter at a new level. But he got no further. The one who betrayed him was at hand.

There are sacrifices for all who work to integrate the opposites and to become mature persons. The Piscean Age asked that death be regarded as a literal, once-for-all event. For the Aquarian person, however, often death, or deaths, are considered to be inner events. Inner deaths are necessary for transformation, for only with the dying of old habits and attitudes can new life come. This acknowledgement of the need for many inner deaths, if transformation is to come, emphasizes the Eighth House of sacrifice in the Aquarian horoscope.

Imagine Jesus' inner feelings when he returned to his disciples for the third time and found them asleep. The great difference between incarnation and vision is exemplified in the difference between Jesus and his disciples. Even though they shared something of Jesus' vision, they were not where he hoped they might be—that is, consciously with him in this moment when "the Son of man was betrayed into the hands of sinners." While Jesus stood there, Judas came and gave him the kiss of death, even as others laid hands on him and took him away. How often have we been overwhelmed with unconsciousness when we need to be conscious people alert to what the moment asks of us.

The first trials of Jesus were before the Jewish authorities. The chief priests and the council sought witnesses to testify against him. Many gave false accounts and their statements did not agree with those made by others; many quoted hearsay and gossip, saying, "we heard it said that he did . . ." The high priest asked Jesus what the witnesses had against him, but he held his peace and said nothing. Then the high priest asked if he were the Christ, the Son of God, and Jesus responded, "Thou hast said." (Matthew 26:64) The high priest rent his garment and said to the people that had heard the blasphemy—what did they think? The people said Jesus was worthy of death.

Jesus was taken to the Roman authorities and delivered to Pilate, who asked him if he were King of the Jews. Jesus answered, "Thou sayest." (Mark 15:2) The chief priests accused him of many things, after which Pilate asked him again, "Answer you nothing?" Jesus did not answer and Pilate marveled. When Pilate found that Jesus had come from Galilee and was under Herod's rule, Pilate sent for Herod who was also in Jerusalem at that time. Herod questioned, Jesus said nothing, and the chief priests and scribes continued vehemently to accuse him. Then Herod sent Jesus back to Pilate.

Jesus' stunning silences leave us in awe of the magnitude of his consciousness. That he did not answer the questions of his accusers has given us a mystery. Even after two thousand years, Jesus' silence and short responses draw us to a deeper awareness of his strategy and words. His answers were not unconscious ambivalence; they were conscious ambiguity. Had he said "yes" or "no," we would not be reading about him now.

Jesus appears to have chosen his destiny, this slow cruel death of being crucified. He might have escaped at the time of Gethsemane, but after his dialogue with God it was clear to him that he was to be killed. Judas was there to give him the kiss of death. Jesus bore the cross until he could no longer carry on and was relieved by Simon of Cyrene. At Golgotha it was placed between the crosses of two thieves who were crucified with Jesus. Roman soldiers were officiating. The women, including Mary Magdalene, were said to be present, but the disciples were not mentioned. If they were at the scene, they were probably not together, but scattered in the crowd or hanging back.

Jesus refused the wine and myrrh that was offered him. This was a Roman execution, and the Roman soldiers cast lots for his garments. There was darkness, perhaps real as well as symbolic, over the whole land. It was a darkness for God, for Jesus, for human kind, for the world; it was darkness of evil.

Jesus is reported to have spoken three times on the cross. The words in Luke, "Father, forgive them; for they know not what they do," and "Father, into thy hands I commend my spirit" (Luke 23:34,46) could have been said by Jesus or they could have been inserted at a later time. One feels there is no doubt, however, about the authenticity of the statement in Mark, which repeats the beginning of Psalm 22: "My God, my God, why hast thou forsaken me?" (Mark 15:34) No one but Jesus could have said these words at this time, and one wonders about the fact that they were allowed to remain in the text. Although this utterance may be the hardest to understand, it is also the most realistic of Jesus' last recorded words, for he had faced the living of his own myth with utmost courage and realism by following the will of God.

From his baptism and wilderness experiences onward, Jesus emphasized the necessity of integrating opposing forces—of bringing opposites together within himself—in order to help

God, who could not do it alone. Consciousness is necessary for such integration. And relationship is how consciousness is developed. God in process knew his need, as we see in his words, "May my mercy overcome my wrath," found in the Midrash. But until the man Jesus declared his commitment to God's will and words, God could not achieve this desired victory of mercy over wrath. Out of the strength of his intimate relationship with God, Jesus went to his death to fulfill both himself and God. At this sacred time of completeness, the evil that killed Jesus was so accepted by him and incorporated into his being for his own fulfillment that he may not have been able to feel God's presence, even though it was most certainly there. It would have been impossible for God not to have been in that very place.

After Jesus' last words, he gave up his spirit, and the veil of the temple was rent in twain from top to bottom. We remember that the heavens were rent asunder at Jesus' baptism. Here we see the tearing of the veil of the temple, the split of the covering of the Holy of Holies in the inner recesses of God's sacred space, which, before, was open only to the high priest. This event brought God's presence to persons at the most intimate level; it has allowed us to enter the holy of holies, into the heart of God. We need to understand this and act on it.

The healing of the split of opposites in God— the division between the evil and the good was a transforming act. But the new religion of that time, Christianity, split the two again, leaving many Christians to see good as the absence of evil. The church sees evil as something that comes to us from the outside. And yet the Genesis myth of our beginnings tells that the Tree of the Knowledge of Good and Evil is planted in the center of the garden along with the Tree of Life. This shows that the knowledge of good and evil is at the center of each of us. To find Life, we need to return to that state of wholeness and reclaim it, which means acknowledging both the good and the evil that are within us. When Jesus talked about life, he was trying to tell us about finding Life from both trees in the garden.

When the evening came, on the day of Jesus' crucifixion, it was the night before the Sabbath. Joseph of Arimathea, who himself was looking for the kingdom of God, asked Pilate for the body of Jesus. Pilate gave the body to Joseph, who wound it in a linen cloth and laid it in a tomb hewn out of rock. Then he rolled a stone against the door of the tomb. It is said that Mary Magdalene and Mary the mother of Jesus observed where he was laid.

Mark, the shortest of the Gospels, ends with the empty tomb of Jesus. Why was the tomb empty? Was the body taken by his friends to a hidden place to protect it? Or was it taken by the ones who killed him in order to prevent trouble over possession of the body? We do not know the answer. It remains part of the mystery.

Although the records of the life of Jesus do not count the disciples as present at the crucifixion, they show Jesus' followers grieving after the postcrucifixion events. In this period of grieving, the disciples, who had been closely with Jesus for some few years, must have had a deep experience similar to Jesus' at the baptism. Because they felt Jesus was alive after his death, they described their experience *as if* Jesus were indeed present. This experience had to have made a great impact on them in order to send them forth to preach a new religion. It was no doubt an experience of God, the Transcendent made Immanent in them. They then called it Jesus. We do not know how long it took before the words "as if he were alive" became, "He is alive."

After this experience of God, the disciples felt ready to go forth and teach what Jesus had been teaching. Their sensitivity to the memory of Jesus, their longing for his presence, no doubt made them susceptible to images of Jesus. These seeming appearances of Jesus were taken as historical reality; it was as if Jesus were alive and in their midst. The disciples believed that if he came once, he would come again, and so they taught others to believe in Jesus the Christ for the remission of sins and eternal salvation.

The people who heard the teachings of the disciples were greatly gripped by the promise that believing in Jesus Christ would take away sins and allow for redemption. Eager to learn of this newly born son of God who brightened life with hope and immortality, the people were filled with joy, regarding their time in history as profoundly significant. One can readily see how this first thousand years after Jesus' death has been called the period of the Christ. During this time, the messianic figure who could atone for one and save those who kept God's commandments captured the psyches of most people in the Western world.

Since astrology was familiar to people in Jesus' time, it is probable that many lived by its knowlege. It was part of their life awareness. Jesus must have known the possibilities of the Aquarian Age, for he had been living those values since his baptism. He also knew his disciples had not been able to actualize the qualities of consciousness he was talking about, even though they had been so closely related to him. Jesus' hope for the understanding of his teaching had to be placed in the future—in this time of the next two thousand years. Now each person needs symbolically to carry his and her own living water; each one of us must be related to our own forgiveness and redemption in relationship to God.

Joachim de Flora, who lived in the eleventh century, made the statement that the Arien Age was the Age of the Father, the Piscean Age was the Age of the Son, and the Aquarian Age is to be the Age of the Holy Spirit. I close with two short poems which seem to summarize the content of this chapter.

Dawn is no longer in the house of the Fish
Pisces, oh Fish, Jesus of the Watery Way,
Your two thousand years are up.

Opening lines from *Astronomical Changes*
by D.H. Lawrence
Collected Works, (Penguin), p. 616

Dawn of the airy age,
the Holy Spirit is with us.
Jesus of Nazareth,
Aquarius is the essence of you.
Your words are here to show the way.
A new two thousand years are yours.

Luella Sibbald

HOW, AS A PSYCHOTHERAPIST I USE ASTROLOGY

Chapter Six

We pick up our horoscope to look at it. We see it is a circle divided into twelve sections with a space in the center.

Besides all the other things this circle of our horoscope symbolizes, it is a mandala, a basic psychic structure occurring frequently in dreams or drawings.

The basic nature of the mandala's fourfoldness is spontaneously manifested, giving a sense of containment and completion—a magic circle of healing. This gives us pause to wonder if the Christian emphasis on the Trinity is adequate.

More than once, when I was working psychologically in the pediatrics ward of a large hospital, I sat in silence beside a child who had been injured seriously in an accident. The child might draw six, eight, ten chaotic drawings and, then, draw a square or a circle with a cross inside. Crooked as those lines might be, that child was striving to contain himself in his own container where healing could take place.

Not only at the physical level did I observe this, but also at the emotional level. One child,

about four, was in the hospital for some minor
reason. Her father, a resident doctor, tucked her
into bed and then had to leave her. She had a
temper tantrum. Any comments by the nurses
such as "You are a big girl now," or "Your daddy
will be back," only made matters worse. She was
given a large stack of drawing paper and
crayons. They were ignored for a while; then she
began frantically to scribble. Her anger, annoy-
ance, despair came out with intensity. I waited.
At last, she drew a circle, divided it into four
parts, handed it to me and smiled. I knew she
had come to a secure place. A very bumpy looking circle is usually a healing act for a small
child. It affirms the child to him herself.

Astrologers have usually taken the center of
the chart to indicate the earth. As my respect
deepens for what a horoscope can mean in self-
knowledge and in self-transformation, I wonder
if possibly the meaning of that center cannot take
on new meaning. It pertains more to our particular time, which asks for greater depth and urges
toward purposeful change.

Not long ago, a woman, not one of my clients
but one whose chart I had done, handed me a
dream she had, saying I could use it in any way I
liked. She is a deeply religious woman, about forty, who has been in analysis for several years.
The dream:

I was trying to meditate. The symbol in front of me was

a mandala fashioned on my astrological chart. The black dot in the center was much larger. All the portions of the mandala were the sections of the chart in marvelous colors and contained other things I can't remember.

Her comments:

> The day before the dream I had been looking at my chart and marvelling at the deep religious significance of it and realized this was at the center of transformation. I saw the black center as representing the deep mystery of the living God. I even painted part of it—all before the dream. It was a deep experience and I felt moved by the wonderful mystery of the union of the individual psyche, the cosmos, and God. Even though the "planets" are in my psyche, there is the profound mystery of patterning in the universe that corresponds to that patterning within my psyche. This was a startling experience. I felt the deeper necessity to know this map of my inner world.

Our dreams come from the place in us that Jung calls the objective psyche (objective because we have no subjective control over it). Therefore, it is a voice other than our conscious one, speaking or revealing in symbolic language. Should we not heed the voice of the Other that comes to us in symbolic language from the objective psyche? How much in our universe has been projected, moved to a new dimension, saved from destruction because this voice, the *Thou*, is heeded? Might there be something for us to ponder from this dream?

Because I use astrology as a tool in my work in psychotherapy, I am basically interested in the birth chart. Charts can be progressed, we can know a great deal about transiting planets, Saturn's returns, and many other subtleties. However, until the person I am working with comes to a truly transformative stage, there is endless material to be absorbed from the birth chart alone. Probably, there are many therapists who use astrology in much this same way. Many of the charts I do are for people working with other therapists. In Europe, most Jungian analysts either work with the chart or are very open to the value it can bring.

One analyst in Europe required clients to have their chart done before he took them. This I don't do. In fact, I don't suggest having the chart drawn. I feel there is an inner wisdom that tells people when to have it done. They hear about it from someone else or in some way it is brought to their attention. When it is interpreted, the frequent comment is, "It is what I am working on in analysis, but now I understand it better."

I used to be quite puzzled by a very provocative question that Dr. Fritz Kunkel, a religious psychologist, asked his seminar groups. The question was "Why did you choose your parents?" It was not until I began observing astrological charts more closely in my psychological work that I felt the reality of this profound question.

When infants come into the world and take that first breath of life, they bring with them a psyche in which the archetypal pattern is already formed. This will determine to a greater or lesser degree the *natural* way that their life will go. Over and over again I observe that people seem to be drawn into homes where the same archetypes, negative and positive, have the greatest possibility of being lived by them naturally.

A person can grow up and say, "If only my mother hadn't made every decision for me," or "If only my father had spent more time with me as a father is expected to, I'd be a different person." The mystery is that the pattern in one's own psyche made it necessary to be in a home where those very situations arose.

But an acorn is not an oak tree. The acorn is the natural seed of the oak, but may always stay an acorn, lost in underbrush, or crushed between rocks. Another acorn may fall on fertile ground, suffer the splitting of its outer shell, and achieve its oak greatness. It has not remained its "natural" self, but has progressed beyond to a supranatural place that expresses the possibility that was there.

Jung has said that to master one's horoscope is to become individuated or to become an integrated person. Marc Edmund Jones, a well-known American astrologer, emphasizes that the myth of the Twelve Labors of Heracles is the myth that represents the birth chart, indicating there is a labor to be accomplished in each house. Both of these statements imply that our birth charts show the "givens" with which we come into the world; and that there is a task to perform, a journey to be taken, if we are to realize the infinite possibilities that exist beyond the givens. This task or journey leads to the refinement of the soul and to the transformation there is to be actualized from the givens.

Scientifically, we know that everything—from the smallest molecule to the great galaxies—has its own unique pattern. The soul, taking its first breath of life, takes on the uniqueness of a movement of time never to be repeated. The fact of individuality is manifest in how persons deal with their life journey. Will they accept the domination of the archetypal pattern and let fate be the determining factor, or will they understand this same patterning so they can relate to it and change the unconscious fate into a conscious destiny? This is all a matter of the choice that each of us must make whether to find our meaning in life or to remain in unconsciousness. Jesus continually stressed choice in emphasizing how to find life rather than destruction.

The patterns in astrology, like the collective unconscious with which Jung's psychology is concerned, consist of symbolic configurations: the planets are the gods, symbols of the power of the unconscious. Or, we could say in Aquarian terms, they are the energies within the psyche with which we will work. The qualities the Zodiac and the planets represent are not personal, but impersonal and objective. The interpretation of the archetypes (the gods or psychic energy) and their interrelationship are the common concerns of both the arts of astrology and psychology.

Eric Neumann, a prominent Jungian, has said:

> The foremost discovery of transpersonal psychology is that the collective psyche—the deepest layer of the unconscious—is the living groundcurrent from which is derived everything I do with a particular ego possessing consciousness. Upon this it is based, by this it is nourished, and without this it cannot exist.

These eternal presences or archetypes are in themselves "non-material" and "invisible." They become "material" and "visible" as archetypal images, i.e., symbols. The structure of the particular psyche determines the gradual manifestation and accentuation of the psychic image of the father. Consequently, we never have just the experience of the personal parent—father or mother—but a complex blend of the actual parent and the archetypal one projected into the reality situation. Thus every actual experience of a parent contains at least two aspects: one, the archetypal image consisting of what we infer from mythic revelation and inner experiences, and two, experiences of our actual parent. The blending of these impersonal and personal factors in each one's psyche are the commonly named archetypes. A few of these archetypes are: mother, father, shadow, anima, animus, hero, animals, wise old man, and wise old woman.

Where do such ideas of the archetypes lead? To assume a natural growth in the psyche (as Jung has done), or an essential truth which life works to fulfill, or an orderly world of collective forms and images, which are the eternal presences, is also to assume a universe in which the totality of the human is *a priori* waiting to be actualized. It is to say God's totality (or the fullness of the gods) is there as divine ground in which it is possible that the direction toward wholeness, and the complete realization of provisional potentials can be actualized. One must assume also a universe wherein a truly cooperative community of humans and the gods or God is essential for the fulfillment of both. The ideas of pre-existent forms and of natural growth derive from the possibility of being able to *discover meaning* rather than to invent it.

As an example, a person had a very weak father who had never been a success and therefore the mother made all the family decisions. In this particular case, the mother had a very profitable job so she was certainly the authority figure in the family. Her concern was to earn a living and to be a strong disciplinarian figure to her children. This mother of my client was rigid, demanding, and had little understanding of her daughter. The actual mother mirrored the pattern of mother that existed in the daughter's collective unconscious. The archetype of the domineering-aggressive mother is thus activiated. The young woman was dominated by this and expected this expression from every feminine authority figure. Being unconscious the archetype was in her, she projected it and brought into reality what she was projecting. Not until she could realize the source of this negativity was in her, in part because of the example of her mother, but more especially because, *a priori*, it also existed in her horoscope (her ego planet was very negatively aspected to the Moon), was she able to become conscious that there is also the opposite in her, the positive mother. Dreams are invaluable in working on the problem. Once she dreamed of her mother as a witch, which indicated the mother, for her, was a more negative, controversial figure than she had realized. Thus the work began in analysis: to reverse this process so that instead of being unconsciously dominated by the archetype of the mother she could relate to it and transform it. She herself was then free as a mother to her children to express the appropriate aspect of the mother to them, instead of the partial negative side that was all she had known.

Sometimes the negative expression is

necessary, but one must be free enough from domination by the inner pattern to choose the appropriate response. This comes when one has experienced each opposite and has come to the integration of them. Through this process one can reach the third point, beyond the opposites, but made up of both.

As far as the individual human psyche is concerned no genuine psychological growth occurs until or unless the rich inner values and potentials of the collective unconscious strata are actualized. This means that they are to be lived in the undramatic nature of everyday life. To be cut off from the unconscious part of the psyche is to be cut off from the "aliveness" of life. It is to live as partial individuals not related to our essential grounding.

Just as every individual has physical organs —heart, lung, kidney, and so forth—likewise, every individual has psychic organs that are common to all. These are the archetypes. The archetypes manifest themselves in all mythologies, fairy tales, religious tradition and dogma, and in ancient mystery cults. What is the myth of the night sea journey but the ancient awareness of the going down each night and rising again each morning of the sun?

The sum of the archetypes signifies for Jung the sum of all latent potentialities of the human psyche—an enormous, inexhaustible store of ancient knowledge concerning the most profound relations between God, the human, and the cosmos. This archetypal world is a powerful influence in our lives. To release its energies, to raise its contents into consciousness, becomes a work and a fulfillment.

The planets, which represent the matrix of the astrological material, have been called by the names of the gods. They represent "heavenly" or religious attributes and archetypal powers. The "gods" need us to express their qualities as part of life. If this is done unconsciously they "possess us," so to speak, and can cause havoc. If, however, we have dealt inwardly with their demands and so understand creatively how they can help us, then there is a relationship that gives its own dimension to life. Like all archetypes, the planets have a positive and negative side. We are emerging from an age that called certain planets malefic and others beneficent. Now we see that they are paradoxical, as is all of life. They each have a positive side and a negative side, but some of the other is always there. Jesus spoke and taught that life was paradoxical. In the Western world it seems to have taken us a long time to begin to realize this truth about life.

For example, if we observe the effects of Mars, the god of war, in our lives, we may experience him through anger or a great play of temper. He may sneak in by that insidious petty way of nagging, but he also manifests in energy, the aggressiveness, or the initiative to start something new. He can be loquacious in an entertaining, witty way or can also be very boring. Mars can be devastating at times if this aggressive-quarrelsome archetype takes over. We must ask ourselves how we have neglected what Mars needs. He longs for activity. We have to propitiate this god by giving outlets to this energy. What activity can satisfy him and not upset the whole household? Perhaps a brisk walk in the country, a bicycle ride, a game of tennis, or even some needlework can give him what he needs and also give us creativity. The more we know ourselves and our inner world, the sooner we feel the rumbles of Martian discontent and find the way to allow the creative things to happen before the storm breaks. How these archetypes are constellated in the individual chart is of the utmost importance, and how we deal with them is the task that confronts us.

In every myth the rising Sun symbolizes coming consciousness. Why do the Navajo face the hogan always toward the east? Instinctively, they want to face in the direction of consciousness. And so in our charts, the east represents where consciousness begins. Jung postulates the ego as the center of the conscious mind. Through our ego consciousness we know about ourselves. An integrated ego, one which has developed without major distortion, is flexible and adjustible. It serves as an organ of assimilation and communication. The ego acts as a mediator between the subject, the I, and the object, the thou, which can be a person, another part of the psyche, or a symbol. The ego should be constantly growing and changing its ways by interaction between itself and others. If one is a growing person the ego becomes more coherent and differentiated through interaction with the non-ego, inner and outer. If the ego identifies with the archetypal content, inflation can result. If the ego is too defended against interaction with others, a rigid ego has developed which can seem well controlled and capable. In reality the rigid ego has achieved a defensive attitude which includes defensiveness against the unconscious in particular. This type of ego is one which rejects new ideas because they are new. On the other hand, if the ego is so loosely controlled as to be incoherent, it is being invaded by contents that cannot be assimilated. In either case, the ego has failed to assimilate the non-ego contents of the unconscious.

It is only through the ego working with the contents of the unconscious (the non-ego) that the Self can be achieved. The ego is the instrument for finding the Self in the process of individuation. Its relation to the dynamics of the work of integration is decisive. The impulse toward integration and consciousness is the great mystery of psychic life representing the inner law and destiny of the psyche.

The First House, the house in the east, represents, in working with a chart, the ego house, The ruler of the rising sign, the Ascendant, becomes the ego planet. More often than not, the ruler of the Ascendant is not always in the First House. In what house it falls, and what planet it is, has much to do with the psychological work that must take place in relation to the psyche.

For example, if the ego planet is in the Tenth House, a house concerned with the outer world and the profession, the person is more concerned, on the whole, with outer events than if the ego planet does happen to fall in the First House, which usually makes one think a great deal about oneself. If the ego planet is in the Eleventh House, relationship in its deepest aspect is usually pursued. And so we could go around the twelve houses. This is making it very general. How the planet is aspected indicates (as a natural result) its effects on a person as positive or negative. We need to realize bringing consciousness to the situation can help how we handle it. What seems very difficult or negative may afterwards find a very positive result. We don't sit around in this world waiting for good days—one acts on what comes.

If the ego planet is Mercury, one feels oneself more on the intellectual side, whether one is a thinking person or not. If the ego planet is Uranus, and at the same time is in the Twelfth House, there is an urgent necessity to explore the unconscious to its depths, giving the ego the expression it needs. A strong but flexible and committed ego determines much about a person's journey in life.

The Seventh House, which pertains to partnership or to marriage, that usually being the most important partnership in one's life, is opposite the First House. The ego house is where we are the most conscious about ourselves, while the Seventh House represents our own other side where we are the most unconscious. In the Seventh House, we are yearning for a constant relationship to that other, to make us whole. The natural sign of Libra enters here in wanting to have the balance that the relation of these two sides would bring. What we are not conscious of in our psyche, we project automatically onto others, and we are well aware most marriages begin with projection. The idealized thou we see in the other is really a part of our own unknown psyche, and in order to be a complete person we need to relate to it in ourselves.

Invariably, if Saturn, Jupiter, or the Sun are in the Seventh House, we project father onto the partner, or in the case of Jupiter, some aspect of the father. This projection doesn't only come from the woman. Many men who may be unusually passive or, because of their own unconsciousness, expect their wives to fulfill the more aggressive functions that one usually expects a father to perform, put the father archetype onto their wives. Likewise, if the Moon is there, one projects motherly qualities onto the marriage partner and/or other acquaintances. Women will generally expect their husbands to be as understanding as mothers should be, whether their own mother was an understanding person or not. They are looking for the positive archetype of the mother.

An example of a heavily emphasized Seventh House is that of a professional man, a lawyer in his middle forties. He is so devoted to his work as to be almost wedded to it.

His house of daily work, the Sixth House, has no planets but is ruled by Mercury, and Mercury is in his Tenth House of profession. This would indicate that his intellect is well involved in his professional activities. Mercury is well aspected with a sextile to both Jupiter and Venus, with a trine to Pluto which gives him a good relation to the unconscious, but with a square to Mars which would have to be watched because he does overdo, leading to emotional and physical strain.

However, in his house of relationship, the seventh, he has Pluto, Mars, Neptune, the Moon, and Jupiter. Because one projects so much from this house of relationship until one knows oneself—it being furthest from the ego house and, therefore, the most unconscious—this shows there is a great deal of work he needs to do in the area of relationship. I commented that Pluto brings change, often death or divorce. He said, yes, each had been true in his marriages. He agreed the divorce had come because he projected all his negativity onto his wife. He was very aware of that now and was watching it. With both the Moon and Jupiter, the mother and qualities of the father must have been projected, I suggested. How well he understood that was what he had done, and he had to watch it at times in his present marriage. Neptune had certainly helped him to idealize and project a spiritual quality onto each partner until the projection began to break and he began to carry that value in himself.

When his third wife died he was quite despairing and decided he could not marry again. He tried being alone for a few years but found it would not work.

His need for companionship, which is indicated by what this house contains, is of great importance to him. He is much in need of relationship. With Jupiter in this house and well aspected, it can mean a very fortunate marriage if he can understand and work with all the archetypes involved and accept that value in himself, rather than projecting it. Both he and his partner in this marriage are in depth analysis, and he is working deeply at making these qualities enrich his own life, instead of expecting them to be carried for him. With the unusual concern and enjoyment of his professional life, he was quite surprised, and yet relieved his chart showed that a satisfactory, creative relationship needed to be achieved and was possible. One hopes he succeeds this time.

The Sun being the day star carries great creative power that is masculine and fiery. Our will, self-confidence, ideals, self-expression, and certainly vitality are contained here. The solar force urges a free expression of one's development.

Mythologically the Sun is related to Apollo, the bearer of light. Also, Dionysus is, or could be, incorporated as the impassioned, intense, unstructured opposite. As this archetype of the masculine is such a potent one, carrying qualities of our self-expression and individuality, to project all these qualities onto a partner, either positively or negatively, is almost too much to bear for the partner. Very frequently this draws people into situations where they work with other people so there is an extended *thou.* Several outstanding Jungian analysts have had this location of the Sun in the Seventh House, including Jung himself. Some people interested in astrology have wanted to make the Sun represent the Self. I do not feel that this is true. The qualities of the Sun, like all the other archetypes expressed in the horoscope, have to be mastered and brought into the unity of the whole person.

The horoscope can be valuable in determining marital difficulties by finding out what each is projecting onto the other. Projection is a valuable tool in understanding our own inner world, for we project those things of which we are unconscious. If we start to work at our partiality by consciously taking the projection back into ourselves, we are becoming a more inclusive person. At the end of the twentieth century most people are still quite vague about this psychological phenomenon that happens to all of us. We may realize how crucial it is to relate to the negative or positive aspect that we are projecting, rather than letting it contaminate the atmosphere. We too often project onto others our negative, unacceptable attitudes we don't want to claim, and thus become infectious. We also do this with our positive qualities, and let someone else carry them, rather than accepting the responsibility for what we are capable of doing.

Two thousand years ago Jesus talked about this psychological fact and warned against it when, in effect, he said, "Why do you see the speck that is in your brother's eye, but do not notice the log that is in your own eye? Or how can you say to your brother, 'Let me take the speck out of your eye' when there is a log in your own eye? You hypocrite, first take the log out of your own eye, and then you will see clearly to take the speck out of your brother's eye." (Matthew 7:3-5 RSV) To work through projections in any relationship, personal or social, leads to growth for all persons concerned and is an important psychological step.

One of the houses of particular interest to me in looking at a chart is the Eighth House. While studying astrology with Gret Baumann-Jung, I found that she called it the house of sacrifice, death, and rebirth. It is Scorpio's natural house, so has always had a great deal to do with life and death. What I learned from her and what has been impressed on me every time I do a chart is the planets in this house, or the planet ruling this house, have something to say about what has been sacrificed in childhood by that person.

For example, just the other day a young woman's horoscope had Sagittarius with its Jupiter ruler as the sign for that house, and the Moon was in the house. I said, "It seems that some aspect of your relationship with your father was sacrificed as a child." She immediately began talking about his drinking habits, his passivity so she never felt the qualities of a normal father. She explained how much he was away from home and that she thoroughly disliked him. Because Jupiter was the planet we were talking about, I asked if the aspect lacking in her father, for her, had also been a religious one. This brought out more intense feeling. He had given up his Catholicism early and therefore had cut himself off from her in any religious communication. Seldom are both parental archetypes in this same house, but with the Moon there, I asked, "Did your mother die at an early age? Or, again, was there a lack of relationship?" The latter had been true. It seemed unbelievable that a mother could have such a lack of understanding, but we have all heard those stories. In one place she said, "She might as well have been dead for all she gave to me as a mother."

A person who has no sense of what a normal father or mother would be like in his life is a very wounded person. It is extremely important the lack that is there, which is the sacrificed part that has been endured, be filled so a rebirth of the father and mother archetype can be achieved. In Goethe's words, "Die to become." To redeem the negative parental archetypes so real transformation in relationship can come is a long inward process and can seldom be done without psychological help. The freedom that comes is more than worth the pain.

Jesus said in one place, "If any one cometh unto me and hateth not his own father and mother . . . he cannot be my disciple. . . ." (Luke 14:25) These are strong words, but Jesus understood what we are just beginning to know today: love and hate are two sides of one attitude. Jesus doesn't want us to hate the parents but images of the parents that are in us, for they are seen by us subjectively according to what we have projected onto them and not objectively as they are. If we find ourselves functioning in life as our mothers did or as our fathers did, which too often is how most people live, then our lives, even as adults, are influenced by our parents too much. If this is true, we have not found our own unique reality and are not truly ourselves. We are reacting to parental images instead of being our own person.

The people to whom I do recommend analysis, if they are not already involved in the process, are those who have a heavily loaded Eighth House. It is especially difficult if one of the planets is the ego planet. Usually young persons with this configuration have so adapted to the attitude of pleasing a parent that they have no realization of what it means to follow their own desires and feelings, or to even know that they have likes or dislikes. Often with Mercury in this house, one discovers that the whole period of childhood, or adolescence if Mars is there, has been sacrificed. The suggestion to people about the sacrifices indicated in the Eighth House brings the most enthusiastic agreement. Some reason has at last been given for the loss of something they couldn't understand, although it has been felt.

Jung has said that no person can be mature without living through childhood and adolescence. It often takes much professional help for an adult to understand how to be father or mother to the inner child so the inner child can grow to be a contributing part of the psyche, rather than a moody, regressive pull-back. Fortunately, a small amount of concentrated time letting that child in us do something "just because," allows the inner child to grow up much faster than the intervening years would indicate. To go for a hike, consciously taking the child with you, and paying attention to what you as a child might have paid attention to, has delight in it and pays off. There are so many ways one can do this. One mother said that when she bought a gift for her outer child, she bought one also for her inner child.

If one does not work analytically in earlier life to restore the sacrificed archetype, often in later life one goes through a psychological death or crisis to restore the sacrificed part. The sacrifices in the Eighth House give such people a particular relation to the oppression and suffering in human life, and to the mystery that has been in their own background, adding often a special relation to the unconscious. This can make them especially helpful in therapeutic relations to others. This house of death also relates to our own death, as well as to inheritances and legacies from the deaths of others.

We all have to pass through the house of death in the second half of life to get to the Ninth House of becoming. This house, which corresponds to Sagittarius, has to do with our outlook on life, our religious attitudes, long voyages, inner and outer. One can have legal encounters with the law of the land, but far more important are encounters with the law of the universe. In this third fiery sign, one is borne into a suprapersonal spiritual reality. In opposition to the Third House, we now become aware of our individual consciousness in relation to inherited conditions. We see here the tendency toward individuation, which generally we will be seeking in the second half of life. It is the period in which we widen horizons. Journeys to foreign lands are the most common way to do this. If you are driven by the spirit and wish to find your own unique religiousness, it can be done through outer travel, to be sure, but also through inner journeying—the way of individuation. This is the process by which the center of the personality shifts gradually away from the ego to the Self. The ego becomes gradually and increasingly aware of the transpersonal archetypal factors involved in the Self, which rules and shapes the personality.

I find more and more people are dissatisfied with religion as they have experienced it in their youth. They are looking for something that speaks to them more individually than do the dogma and creeds of organized religion. Jung has said that if people are contained in the church, it is important they remain there. On the other hand, if the dogma and authoritarian structure no longer answer their need, they must be true to that and find themselves in their own religious way through journeying into the unconscious. Though dogma and creed originally emerged from authentic religious experiences of

the unconscious, their formalization into structures tends to constrict. This makes the possibility of an individualized religious experience very
difficult, if not impossible. Many people today are
seeking for new religious expression.

Because the Eleventh House is the natural
Aquarian house, it needs some mention. It is the
house of friendship, and of fulfilled wishes and
desires. The Aquarian symbol of the mature person holding a water jar from which flows the living water of life would indicate the Aquarian concern for humanity. The water is pouring forth for
the needs of those less fortunate.

As the only other human beings used as Zodiacal symbols, the Gemini twins are youthful, as
is also the virgin, the symbol of Virgo. With an
adult person as its symbol, we can thus assume a
wholeness about Aquarius which is not only possible to achieve, but which also indicates maturity in the true sense. This wholeness comes from
the integration of the conscious and the unconscious; the uniting of the opposites. This
leads to the achievement of the Self, or the image
of God within, as Jung would say. Freud
rediscovered the unconscious and Jung added to
what Freud began by postulating the collective
unconscious. The person who is in the process of
uniting the opposites to achieve the Self finds his
or her own living water, or the redeeming quality
within, which is poured out in service to others.
This Eleventh House of friendship is one in

which inner values and spiritual values prevail.

Friendships have this connotation of people most deeply related as friends, when they are working together for a common value. We see how this group archetype is moving in our time, often still too unconsciously, in the many communes and group activities that are being tried out. Some of them are lasting. Many groups are disillusioned and give up. It may be the Aquarian group process will not truly work unless the first step has been accomplished of becoming a more whole person who understands the inner opposites; this understanding includes one's shadow side and those qualities one has pretended are not present in one's psyche.

Let us look now at the Twelfth House which I feel, along with the Eighth House, needs a great deal of introversion to give the psyche its true value. It refers to that which is hidden. Lying as it does back of the First House, the ego house, it can manifest the relationship of the unconscious of the person to the ego. It is often related to the part of ourselves we are not brave enough to accept and face. It is a channel for intuition, inspiration, and the most mystical or spiritual values if we work to bring them out of their hiddenness, corresponding to the original sign of the Twelfth House—Pisces.

It is a house that emphasizes the need to go inward. We must meet the inner enemies that undermine our being lest we have to meet them outwardly. This introverted attitude can make one seem asocial, but it is the necessary condition for meeting the pushed-aside energies in us, the neglected gods, in order to let them function in our psyche, which needs to be inclusive of all qualities. Jesus, in effect, said, "You must be all-inclusive as your heavenly Father is all-inclusive." (Matthew 5:48) This means accepting the positive and negative as part of ourselves.

If this Twelfth House happens to be a heavily emphasized house, to ignore the demands the unconscious is making could mean to fall ill, or to be so perverted as to commit some criminal act.

Persons who have chosen to enter a monastery or convent often have a Twelfth House that has several planets in it, for this retreat from the world helps to insure the necessary solitude that is unconsciously felt when a Twelfth House is heavily occupied.

Rainer Maria Rilke, the poet, was one who had many planets in this house. In spite of some very deep relationships, he lived much alone. During one of these periods of aloneness he wrote the "Duino Elegies" in which he worked through the problems of his life in his own introverted way. The use of the familiar "Du" in the original manuscript would indicate how much he was writing to other parts of himself, unconcerned if others ever read it or not.

I have often found the planet in this Twelfth House, the one manifested only when the person goes into solitude and the unconscious, is often related to some part of life not lived in any reality by the parents. And more often than not, it is also true it was not lived by the generation preceding the parents (if they knew their grandparents well enough to be able to tell).

Frequently this unlived planet seems to be either the Moon or Venus, though I have done no statistical work to prove this. The person in whose chart either of these planets falls in the Twelfth House usually admits the mother was very lacking in passing on any motherly feelings or anything about feminine relationship values or the expression of them. Often it was just as true of her mother's mother. If it is a man, he feels lacking in his inner feminine feelings. It seems as if these particular people have a "karmic debt" to past generations to relate to the value of that ignored archetype to bring it into a reality that must be lived by them. It could be possible that the thousands of years of emphasis on a patriarchal Godhead in the Hebrew Scriptures and Christianity have buried the natural expression of the feminine and it is showing now in the horoscope as something to be worked on inwardly, just as it is obviously a dominating issue in the outer world today.

One person with several planets in her Twelfth House, among which was Uranus, her ego planet (she had Aquarius rising), realized her need to go deeply into the unconscious. Uranus, as a planet related to the unconscious, was asking for much solitude and inner work. Because she responded with devotion and concentration to Uranus' needs, her already developed talent for writing was reinforced from the collective unconscious in a very intuitive, irrational, creative way. The ego was only slightly involved in this process, for the talent for writing had become the servant of the larger whole, the Self. The ego was unaware what the next episodes of her novels were to be. These episodes unfolded as she wrote, coming from the unknown source of the deep collective unconscious. These results were manifested by a mature person who had worked deeply in analysis, as well as with her spiritual life, for many years. This does emphasize the treasures to be found in the unconscious if the work is done to uncover those treasures. The seed of some unknown talent may be found adding much to one's life and to the greatly needed consciousness of the world.

I have been stressing the houses in which I may take a slightly different point of view from one or another of the more traditional views of those working with the astrological chart. However, it has been what really works in helping to go deeper into therapy. The emphasis that I have been pointing out seems to help the analysands feel more aware of the reality of the tasks they are working with in analysis so they can become more conscious people.

The Second House, that of money, possessions, and feeling, does indicate a certain relationship to one of the parents. As money is symbolic of energy, the ruler of the sign of this
Second House, or the planet in it, (depending on
its being a masculine or a feminine planet), indicates usually whether it was the father or the
mother who gave the individual the energy to
move into life. It can indicate it was that parent
who was the most related and concerned and the
most encouraging; or, negatively, it can be the individual moved into life to escape that particular
parent's influence. It is a helpful indication of the
existence of a certain parental attitude, either
positive or negative.

I remember one woman who so belittled herself that she never spoke in a public situation.
She never offered suggestions. She was so retir-
ing it was hard to feel her reality, though she was
more than willing to serve under someone else's
initiative. She was in analysis and the analyst
urged her to have her horoscope cast.

I was amazed to see what an excellent Third
House she had, the house that speaks of one's
intellectual gifts. In it, she had the Sun, Uranus,
and Mercury. She herself would hardly believe it
and could not accept what it could mean to her.
The sign ruling this house was Pisces, the sign of
Christianity, which is inclined to make some people feel guilty if they give to themselves instead of
to others. Her home environment had emphasiz-

ed her serving in a kindly way, which is a limited aspect of Pisces, far from the positive artistic qualities and illumination that also go with the sign. She had really been sacrificed to her environment and could not see herself acting independently. Because of many fixed signs in the rest of her chart, it was a long struggle for her and the analyst to get her to accept the responsibility of the creativity she had. The metamorphosis has come. She has emerged much more of a leader than a server and is a very alive person, heading committees and taking initiative. I don't believe this would have been possible without the visible evidence of this particular potential in the Third House and other creative elements leading into it.

The Fourth House usually indicates which parent, or possibly grandparent, the person is more like in looks and disposition. From this Fourth House, one can determine often how rooted in their own being individuals are. Can they handle the difficulties found in the rest of the chart? This is a very open question and indicates the mystery of the quality of the individual, a mystery I am very grateful is there. The unknowns in the uniqueness of each individual make it impossible to truly anticipate what a person will be like who sits before you, even though you see many possibilities from a study of the horoscope. This keeps the therapist open, fluid, and flexible, a most necessary attitude.

I have not mentioned the archetypes representing the contrasexual portion of the psyche, the
anima for the man and the animus for the
woman. Jung speaks of them as the soul images
of each, respectively. The anima is made up partly by the man's personal relation to his mother
and partly by all experience of the opposite sex,
so the Moon, Venus, and Neptune, and how they
are aspected to each other, would indicate a great
deal about how his anima is for him. Likewise the
woman's animus is constituted by her experience of her father and partly by all other experiences of masculinity. There are many more
masculine planets that can shape the quality and
functioning of the animus. To accomplish a
creative relationship to either the anima or
animus is one of the most important tasks in
therapy.

Because Jung has said that basically every
neurosis is religious in origin, I am always interested in Jupiter, for, among other qualities
Jupiter indicates the religious archetype,
whether it is in the Ninth House having to do
with religious attitudes, or elsewhere. More and
more I find religious expresssion is basically an
individual expression, rather than being related
to the structure of a church. At least this seems
true of the people whom I contact.

As we move into the last years of the Piscean
Age, the religious archetypes of that age do not

contain the unconscious psyche of persons;
already there is a reaching toward something
new geared to the energy of an inner reality for
each individual. Since the beginning of the scien-
tific outlook around the time of the Renaissance,
science has been seen more materialistically.
Everything had to be proven, documented,
witnessed. Today we hear many outstanding
scientists like Pauli, Bohr, Oppenheimer, Port-
mann and many less known say the further they
proceed into science, the more they have to ad-
mit that some purpose, or meaning, or in other
words—God—has to be a basic premise. No longer
among the leaders working in these fields is there
such a split between science and religion, though
it may take generations for others to catch up
and understand this fact.

The same phenomenon is true in the area of
myth. We used to say myth is something that is
not true because we have not seen those things in
reality, or else myth describes miracles. Today,
because of the rediscovery of the unconscious,
we know that every myth, whether the Genesis
creation myth, the Navajo, or the Japanese, or
any other creation myth, is psychological truth
and therefore has reality. It explains how things
happen in the inner world, which people felt inwardly thousands of years ago and told from
generation to generation. At last these oral traditions were written for us to relate to as events
that happen inwardly. As we become aware of

this, we become conscious of our unconscious contents, and are moving toward being more integrated people.

All of this has a great deal to do with the fact the Christian archetypes seem no longer sufficient to contain the religious life for many people. If one studies the three Synoptic Gospels in a critical way, it is quite possible the material about Jesus which is historical can be distinguished from what is nonhistorical. Minimal as the material is, one can be grateful there is enough evidence to let us see the man Jesus and his teaching emerge differently from what Christianity has taught us. (The Gospel of John is a philosophical book and very important but is not taken to be historical by scholars.) Jesus was a person steeped in his Jewish heritage which he moved beyond, just as his far-sighted teaching differs from the outreach of Christianity. Therefore, what he taught speaks in a way very relevant to us today, as the archetypes of the new age move to be understood and lived. (This subject was dealt with in more depth in the Fifth Chapter, but I am letting this portion remain as it appeared in this paper when given as a lecture.)

At no time in his life did Jesus of Nazareth identify outwardly with the messianic concept or, as the Greek word expressed it, with the Christ concept. When his disciples called him the Christ, he talked about the Son of man who must suffer many things and be rejected by the established religion of the time. When, at the trials, he was asked, "Art thou the Christ?" he answered the Jewish and Roman authorities with the same, "Thou hast said." It seems evident this was a very conscious ambiguity on his part. He implied many times that if he could become a Son of man by living life in relationship to God, it was also possible for others to achieve the same relationship if they followed his teaching.

However, early Christianity was founded on the symbol of him as the risen Christ who will come again, and to believe in him was to be redeemed and saved. It was a religion about Jesus not the religion of Jesus. Jesus himself seldom used the word "believe." He knew one had to experience rather than to believe.

The life of Jesus was one of dealing with the opposites and integrating them into his own wholeness until at his crucifixion he faced ultimate evil and took it into himself for his fulfillment. However, the Christian Christ has become a very one-sided concept representing only the light side. The two Piscean fishes going in different directions reopened the split between good and evil which Jesus, as a prototype of what is possible, had healed.

So after almost two thousand years of trying to identify with the Christ figure, we have disowned our own darkness and evil, have pushed them into the unconscious and then projected them onto our family, our neighbors, other nations and races, and into the world in general.

The rediscovery of depth psychology makes us realize the darkness and evil lurking in the unconscious, along with all the treasure and potential also buried there, must be brought together into a unity or wholeness within each one of us. Jung calls this wholeness the Self, or the *imago Dei*, the image of God within.

Then, mature persons, carrying their own living water of redemption which they pour forth in service to others, will actualize in the world the hope which is in the symbol of Aquarius. The "second coming" is this consciousness of the Self within each one, who integrates the opposites, both light and dark, masculine and feminine, and all others that have been split apart. When this has been achieved, communities of individuals can live together in a creative way. We see the archetype of this quality moving in the communes attempted today. As I have said above, some are succeeding; others are not because there is still too much unconsciousness about the inner opposites that must be integrated to find the transforming third point beyond which is the expression of the Self.

We all give lip service to the fact that we must know ourselves. As Jung has asked, "How many, indeed, find this necessity binding upon themselves ?" Nicholas of Cusa, one of the early mystics, has God say, "Know thyself and I shall be thine." When we know ourselves by going into the depth of the unconscious, we know God and we help God to know Him/Herself.